The One-Stop Guide to World Religions

THE
ONE-STOP
Guide to
World Religions

Hugh P. Kemp

LION

Published by Lion Books
an imprint of
Lion Hudson plc
Wilkinson House, Jordan Hill Road,
Oxford OX2 8DR, England

ISBN 978-0-7459-5509-4
First edition 2013

Acknowledgments

Special thanks go to Colin Edwards for writing the section on Islam. I would also like to thank Ali Hull of Lion, along with the team of editors who have been patient with me in meeting deadlines. Thanks too to my eldest daughter (and recent graduate in philosophy), Anjali Kemp, who worked as my research assistant during parts of this project. My long-suffering wife Karen and daughters deserve extra praise for sticking with me through it! Thanks!

Text acknowledgments

Christian Scripture quotations taken from the Holy Bible, New International Version, copyright © 1973, 1978, 1984 International Bible Society. Used by permission of Hodder & Stoughton, a member of the Hodder Headline Group. All rights reserved. "NIV" is a trademark of International Bible Society. UK trademark number 1448790.
p. 77: Extract from *Mere Christianity* by C.S. Lewis copyright © C.S. Lewis Pte. Ltd. 1942, 1943, 1944, 1952. Reprinted by permission.
p. 83: The Lord's Prayer as it appears in Common Worship: Services and Prayers for the Church of England (Church House Publishing, 2000) is copyright © The English Language Liturgical Consultation and is reproduced by permission of the publisher.
p. 112: Text from Linda Edwards' *A Brief Guide to Beliefs*, used by permission of Westminster John Knox Press.

A catalogue record for this book is available from the British Library
Printed and bound in China, July 2013, LH06

Contents

Introduction 7

Theory and Background 8
DEFINING WORLD RELIGIONS

Mapping the World's
Religions 10

Primal Religion 12
PRIMITIVE BELIEFS

Ancient Civilizations 14
MESOPOTAMIA AND BABYLON

Egypt 16
GETTING READY FOR DEATH
AND THE AFTERLIFE

Greece and Rome 18
GRECO-ROMAN RELIGION

Northern Europe 20
THE CELTS AND THE GERMANIC TRIBES

Indus Valley
Civilization 22
HARAPPANS AND ARYANS

African Religion 24
DIVERSITY AND COMMUNITY

Shamanism 26
RELIGION OF ECSTACY

Pacifica and Australian
Aboriginal 28
MELANESIAN, MICRONESIAN,
AND POLYNESIAN

Native American
Religion 30
NATURAL AND SPIRITUAL WORLDS

The Peoples of
the Andes 32
THE INCAS

Hinduism 34
A WAY OF LIFE 34
LITERATURE OF THE HINDUS 36
THE KEY IDEAS 38
SOCIETY AND VILLAGE LIFE 40
INFLUENCE IN THE WEST 42

Buddhism 44
THE LIFE OF THE BUDDHA 44
A GLOBAL RELIGION 46
THE FOUR TRUTHS AND BUDDHIST
TEXTS 48
SECTS AND MOVEMENTS 50
A WESTERN PHENOMENON 52

Chinese Religions 54
THE THREE TEACHINGS

Daoism 56
TEACHERS AND HISTORICAL
DEVELOPMENT 56
MAIN IDEAS AND INFLUENCE 58

Confucianism 60
CONFUCIUS THE MAN 60
KEY IDEAS, TEACHINGS, THE *ANALECTS* 62
THE LEGACY IN CHINA 64

Judaism 66
HISTORICAL FOUNDATIONS AND
OVERVIEW 66
THE PATRIARCH, MOSES 68
BELIEF 70
RITUAL AND ACTION 72
MODERN JUDAISM AND THE STATE 74

Christianity 76
THE CENTRALITY OF JESUS 76
ITS ESTABLISHMENT AND SHAPE 78
THE BIBLE 80
BELIEF AND PRACTICE 82
GOING GLOBAL 84

Islam 86
INTRODUCTION AND DEFINITIONS 86
MUHAMMAD 88
THE HOLY SCRIPTURES 90
BELIEFS AND PRACTICES 92
SUNNI, SHI'A, AND SUFI 94

Yoruba Religion
and Voodoo 96
FROM AFRICA TO THE WORLD

Jainism 98
A PEACEFUL RELIGION

Zoroastrianism 100
AND THE PARSEES OF MUMBAI

Sikhism 102
GURU NANAK, BELIEF,
AND THE *GURUDWARA*

Japanese Religion
and Shinto 104
OLD RELIGION IN A MODERN STATE

Bahai 106
UNITY OF ALL

Mormonism 108
CHURCH OF JESUS CHRIST
OF LATTER DAY SAINTS

Paganism 110
ANCIENT RELIGION IN A NEW AGE

Postmodernity 112
CHALLENGE TO RELIGION

Atheism, Secularism,
and Unbelief 114
NO NEED FOR GOD

Revivals and Renewal
Movements 116
NEW RELIGIOUS MOVEMENTS

New Age Movement
and Esoterica 118
MAKING LIFE SACRED AGAIN

Fundamentalism 120
EXTREME RELIGION

Bibliography 123

Index 124

Picture Acknowledgments
127

Introduction

A quick flick through a history book reminds us that "religion makes the world go around". So much good has come of religion throughout history: it has been the expression of humankind's longing for significance and the divine; religious impulses have been expressed in the world's greatest literature and art; it has motivated men and women to aid the poor and the marginalized, get rid of slavery, stand for truth, and work for a just world.

However, religion is often in the news for negative reasons. In an age in which there is so much violence attributed to religion, it is necessary for us to learn about each other's beliefs and rituals: we need to remind ourselves of the good in religion, but also face up to its darker expressions. This doesn't mean we give up our treasured beliefs and convictions, nor do we give up our debates about ultimates. Good conversations come out of well-informed minds, stirred by hearts that desire the best for others. It is my desire that this book, a small contribution to a wealth of writing on the subject of world religions, will aid readers in gaining a better understanding of the many and varied religious expressions that make us who we are.

Apart from the chapters on Islam (written by Colin Edwards), the words that follow are my own, although I have drawn on the works of others. My own convictions are Christian, but I was born in India among that amazing melting pot of religions. I have worked in Asia, and studied Christianity, history, sociology, and Buddhism at graduate level.

The structure represents my own interests and experiences. I've tried to select the "biggies" – the main religions that we meet every day – and then the "significant others" – those that also shape the world in which we live. I also address some of today's challenges to religion, such as the impact of postmodernism and the increasing secularization of society.

Studying religion can sometimes make you feel as though you are caught in a tumble drier: it seems like a topsy-turvy experience. However, this perhaps is the nature of religions – they are about real people seeking answers to messy questions, with gods, rituals, symbols, stories, and ideas that speak to the human longing for meaning and purpose. It is this that binds us together as humans, and by understanding each other better we can, I hope, ultimately learn to accept our varied and different belief systems.

Hugh P. Kemp

Theory and Background

DEFINING WORLD RELIGIONS

Humans can't help but be religious. Religions come in a huge variety of forms, and there are many ways of studying them. Increasing globalization, along with the rapid technological developments of the twenty-first century, have led to more communication than ever before between people of different faiths and cultures; it is therefore important that we gain an understanding of the religious traditions that influence people's worldviews.

What, then, is religion? What might a "world" religion be? How should we talk about religion? Some religions are very old, conservative, and resistant to change. Others are new, innovative, and constantly re-inventing themselves.

What is Religion?

Religion is a quest for an ideal existence, a seeking beyond oneself for meaning in life. Some say that the quest itself defines what religion is; others say that the quest has both an end and an answer. Most (but not all) "religions" claim some knowledge of, and relationship with, the divine or the spiritual, often in the form of gods or an ultimate God.

Religion takes shape in rituals, beliefs, and institutions, such as worship and the writing and compiling of scriptures. These give order and shape to identity, offer a sense of community, and help us to experience the divine. Religion regulates ethics: it answers the question, "How should I live?" Some religions are shaped by circumstances and their moment in history. Others claim to be revelations – the god reveals characteristics, codes for living, and even their personality to humans.

Religion: Dead or Alive?

With the rise of science from the sixteenth century, there has been growing talk of the death of God, the irrelevance of religion, and the increasingly secular nature of society. However, people do not seem to want to allow religion to die, and new religious movements have emerged, often reinterpreting old traditions, and mixing and matching a variety of elements from different faiths.

In Asia, for example, religion is alive and well. Confucianism and ancient Brahmanism (now Hinduism) have influenced the worldviews of millions of people in both China and India. With deep worldview roots in the soil of Pacifica, Africa, Asia, and South America, indigenous peoples are now finding a stronger voice through explicit political representation and growing self-identity. Today, these ancient religions find themselves with both opportunities and new challenges.

How Do We Recognize A Religion?

When seeking to study a religion, where might we start, and how might we go about it? Scholar Ninian Smart (1927–2001), in his *The World's Religions* (1989), suggests there are seven dimensions to religion.

1. The practical and ritual dimension. What rituals are performed? Some examples include Passover, circumcision, Hajj, ceremonial washing, and kissing an icon.

2. The experiential and emotional dimension. How do I feel? What do I experience? Do I feel more holy? How am I emotionally connected and affected by this religion? What emotions might visions and dreams arouse in me?

3. The narrative or mythic dimension. What stories and scriptures do I find helpful? What is the overarching "story" that we all agree on (for example, a creation story)?

4. The doctrinal and philosophical dimension. Where does authority lie? How do I understand reality? What beliefs do I subscribe to? Why do we believe and practise these things?

5. The ethical and legal dimension. How should I live? What is right and wrong?

6. The social and institutional dimension. What institutions give this religion its shape? Marriage? Church governance? How is the community organized? Who leads and why?

7. The material dimension. Where do people meet (temples, churches)? What material things do we use: prayer beads, images, candles? What makes something holy?

These seven dimensions offer a broad base for describing any religion. Ninian Smart later added two more, political and economic: how might a religion relate to the wider society of which it is a part? What is its relationship to the state and the economy?

It may be wise to add a tenth dimension: natural/creation/environmental. This might include questions like, what might this religion say about how we care for the world around us?

Far left: A Maharashtrian Indian bride and groom's wedding ceremony.
Left: Muslim worshippers at Friday prayers at the Nakhoda Mosque, Kolkata, West Bengal, India.

Religion Has "Family Resemblances"

The problem of definition plagues religion. What about Marxism? Secularism? Paganism? Are these religions? Like family members who look similar, we can think of religions as having "family resemblances". The influential philosopher Ludwig Wittgenstein (1889–1951) came up with this idea. For example, two religions as different as Christianity and Hinduism have family resemblances in that members of both religions do acts of worship to a deity, and there are initiation and washing rituals, to name a few. These acts of worship can be formalized and informal acts of devotion to a deity, a "hero/heroine" or a saint. Often these may be images. In addition, the priority of a female image or the elevation of feminine qualities could be considered to be a "family resemblance". Above, a Christian worshipper kisses the hand of the Virgin of Macarena in Seville, Spain.

Mapping the World's Religions

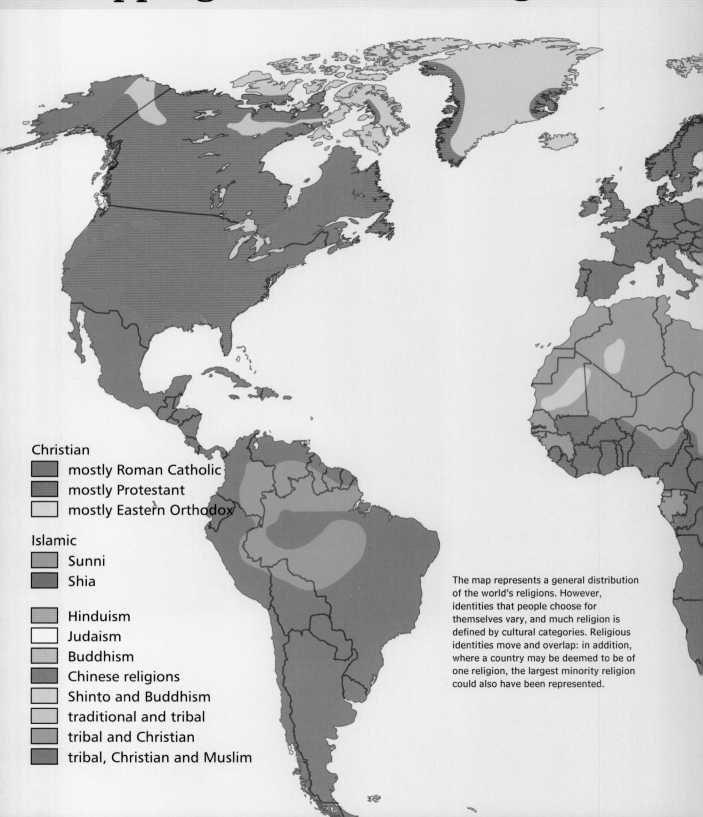

Christian
- mostly Roman Catholic
- mostly Protestant
- mostly Eastern Orthodox

Islamic
- Sunni
- Shia

- Hinduism
- Judaism
- Buddhism
- Chinese religions
- Shinto and Buddhism
- traditional and tribal
- tribal and Christian
- tribal, Christian and Muslim

The map represents a general distribution of the world's religions. However, identities that people choose for themselves vary, and much religion is defined by cultural categories. Religious identities move and overlap: in addition, where a country may be deemed to be of one religion, the largest minority religion could also have been represented.

Primal Religion

PRIMITIVE BELIEFS

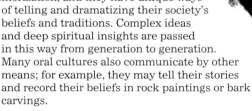

Most world religions have holy texts: for example, Christianity has the Bible; Islam, the Qur'an; Hinduism, the Gita; and Sikhism, the Granth Sahib. But what about those societies without a tradition of writing? Many societies in the world are non-literate or oral, that is, they communicate chiefly by the spoken word, and their traditions are memorized.

Oral Traditions

The religion of oral societies has tended to be viewed as magic or superstition, with the implication that these religions were undeveloped, unsystematic, and hence not really noteworthy. An ... v suggests that perhaps religion has "evolved" over millennia, and these oral societies are in a sense "primitive".

But this isn't necessarily the case. Non-literate oral societies have quite sophisticated belief systems, with complex rituals and profound mythology and symbolism. In other words, just because a people is non-literate, it does not mean they do not have a noteworthy religion. Members of non-literate oral cultures have extraordinary powers of memorization, and they have unique ways of telling and dramatizing their society's beliefs and traditions. Complex ideas and deep spiritual insights are passed in this way from generation to generation. Many oral cultures also communicate by other means; for example, they may tell their stories and record their beliefs in rock paintings or bark carvings.

Animism

"Primal" religion is the best of a poor selection of words for the beliefs of these oral cultures. Primal religion contains basic, fundamental, even universal religious forms. More literate religions have some characteristics of primal religion, such as the idea of the interconnectedness of humanity with the world, and the concept of an intermediary figure between humankind and the gods. In addition, the term "primal religion" implies a sense of "first-ness": it precedes and informs whatever follows. It does imply an evolutionary model of the development of religion (something that is debated); nevertheless, the term allows various religions to stand in their own right.

Primal religions are usually grouped together as "animism". All physical things have *anima* (Latin for "life", "soul"), and are animated by spirit. These societies believe that the material and spiritual worlds are one and the same: everything has *anima*, that is, everything is *animated* by having a living soul of some sort.

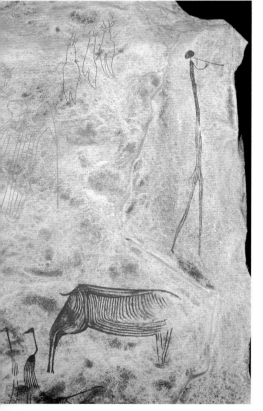

Above: A lion mask of a shaman of the Ashanti tribe, Africa. This type of mask is used by medicine men in village ceremonies. It may be used for animal transformation during specific initiatory rites or simply symbolizes strength and courage.

Left: Later Stone Age Tanzanian rock painting interpreted by recent scholars as recording a shamanistic trance dance known as *simbo*. A shaman in trance is depicted with the sensation of bodily elongation and nasal bleeding. The blood was seen as the boiling up of potency and was used in healing.

● SEE ALSO
SHAMANISM PP. 26–27
AUSTRALIAN ABORIGINAL PP. 28–29
NATIVE AMERICAN RELIGION PP. 30–31
YORUBA RELIGION PP. 96–97

CHARACTERISTICS OF PRIMAL RELIGION

Ninian Smart (1927–2001) was a leading scholar and teacher in the field of Religious Studies. In his book *The Religious Experience of Mankind* (1984), he sets out some of the main features of primal religion.

MANA

A term originating in the cultures of the Pacific, *mana* is a surrounding force that is invisible and populated with deities. *Mana* resides in chieftains, animals, places, and large rocks or geographical features of significance.

TAPU TABOO

From the Pacific word *tapu*, it is the idea that someone is so full of *mana* that they cannot be approached by the profane and worldly. Things also may be taboo, or a taboo may be put on something, setting it aside as "holy". A warrior on the eve of battle may become ritually taboo, and a corpse may be taboo, for example.

HIGH GOD

Most, if not all, primal religions have a concept of a High God. The High God is above and beyond this world; it is creator and ruler of all, including souls. The High God is often regarded as remote and can't be described; hence people pay greater attention to lower gods.

TOTEMISM

Rooted in the natural world, totemism relates to kinship with animals or a species of plant. The totem object is sacred: perhaps it is heroic in legend or is the creator of the tribe. The totem animal usually represents strength, cunning, or wisdom.

ANCESTOR VENERATION

The human creator of the society, or a hero with great mana, is often honoured through religious ritual. This may be done due to perceived connections with fertility and the health of the land. Ancestors live on; they are the "living-dead".

SHAMAN

A shaman is a person with the gift of ecstasy who can go between the living and the "living-dead". The motif of journey is important: the shaman has powers to journey to the realm of the living-dead so as to return with guidance, healing, and wisdom.

Myth

• • • • • • • • • • • • • • • • • •

Myth and storytelling are important in primal religions both in their content, and the ongoing pattern of their telling. Myths explain origins, good and evil, local landforms, past events, and future possibilities.

THE CREATION MYTH OF THE MONGOLS

This myth comes from *The Secret History of the Mongols* (thirteenth century), as translated by Igor de Rachewiltz (2004).

> *In the beginning there was a blue-grey wolf, born with a destiny ordained by Heaven Above. He mated with a fallow doe and together they came across the Tengis lake, and settled at the source of the Onan river, on Mount Burhan Kaldun. And Batachkhan was born…*

The Atlantean figures of Tula de Allende, Mexico, represent fierce Toltec warriors, immortalized from the pre-Aztec Tula culture (AD 800–1000). Making statues of ancestors serves a similar purpose to totemic animals: they represent strength, wisdom, and guardianship.

Ancient Civilizations

MESOPOTAMIA AND BABYLON

Although archaeologists classify ancient civilizations in a number of different ways, one of the main characteristics is that they generally formed on or near river basins, or other sources of water. From 3500 BC onwards, Mesopotamia (modern Iraq), the Yellow River (China), the Indus Valley (modern Pakistan), and the Nile River (Egypt) all became home to four well-recognized ancient civilizations.

Each ancient civilization established its own culture, systems of government, agricultural practices, and social hierarchies. Throughout history, as civilizations have risen and fallen, they have provided the world with the basis for its cultural foundations: for its writing, mathematics, governments, engineering, economics, philosophy, and religion.

The generative power of water – and consequently fertility – was often a theme in a civilization's culture. Over time, city-states formed, supported by an agricultural hinterland. The gods were believed to control nature, particularly the rising and falling of the river, and hence fertility. Water represented both chaos and order. Fertility was often personified in the role of the king or queen, who was considered divine in some sense.

Mesopotamia

There is much in common in the ancient religions of Mesopotamia: they are all derived from the ancient Sumerians and Akkadians who were the first cultures to dominate Mesopotamia – *meso potamos* – the place "between the rivers". This is the long, broad, fertile valley of the Tigris and Euphrates rivers in modern Iraq. It is one of the ancient cradles of civilization.

EMPIRES THAT HAVE INHABITED MESOPOTAMIA

- Sumeria and Akkadia (3500–608 BC): the first cultures to make their mark

- Assyria (2300–612 BC): city-states, with Nimrod and Nineveh being dominant

- Babylon (1900s–500s BC): Babylon fell in 539 BC

- Persia (550–331 BC): extended from India to Greece.

LITERATE CIVILIZATIONS

The civilizations that rose and fell in Mesopotamia were built around city-states. They were urban, and their religion reflected this. While they are now "extinct" religions, the Mesopotamian civilizations have left a legacy of religious artefacts. Cuneiform writing, for example, was born in Sumer: it is therefore perhaps the earliest culture in which we can read of their religious beliefs. Legal codes have been discovered (particularly that of Hammurabi), which shed light on the religions of later peoples; for example, it is reasonable to suggest that the Ten Commandments of the Old Testament are structured on the legal codes of Mesopotamia. There are also several stories of a great flood throughout Mesopotamia, one of which is in the Bible. Above, a map of the Mesopotamian world with cuneiform inscription. Babylon is in the centre and Assyria and Elam are also named. The central area is ringed by a circular waterway.

Map shows the location of ancient civilizations of the world.

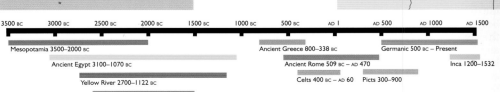

3500 BC	3000 BC	2500 BC	2000 BC	1500 BC	1000 BC	500 BC	AD 1	AD 500	AD 1000	AD 1500

Mesopotamia 3500–2000 BC

Ancient Egypt 3100–1070 BC

Yellow River 2700–1122 BC

Indus Valley 2650–1500 BC

Ancient Greece 800–338 BC

Ancient Rome 509 BC – AD 470

Celts 400 BC – AD 60

Picts 300–900

Germanic 500 BC – Present

Inca 1200–1532

The Mesopotamian Gods

The Mesopotamian cultures had many gods. An was the supreme god, but Enlil, the god of air/wind, was the better known. The wind brought rain, which nourished crops. Ancient Mesopotamians believed that land "floated" on an ocean, and that springs and wells were evidence of this. Rain and irrigation ultimately produced wealth. But wind and rain could also be destructive. Enlil held the tablets of fate: his female consort is Ninlil, or Lady Wind. Enki is the god of the underground waters, and is crafty and fun.

Fertility, and by implication immortality, is a dominant theme in ancient religions. Ishtar is the Akkadian goddess of fertility: in Assyria she is Astarte. Again, associated with nourishment in water, she is the goddess of showers and thunderclouds, and also the goddess of war. Marduk is the god of thunderstorms and he represents fertility as a young bull. Chaos always lurks near, and much in Mesopotamian religion is the quest for order, because of the threat of the world turning to chaos through out-of-control water in the form of storms and floods. Order is needed so that both agriculture and urban society are successful. It follows that creation myths relate the bringing of order out of chaos: the created order is always threatened by the return of the world to a watery grave.

Babylonian Creation

Creation according to the Babylonians comes out of conflict. Tiamat was the goddess who tried to destroy the other gods, but Marduk killed her. He then cut her in two, and used these to create heaven and earth. Tiamat's tears are the Tigris and Euphrates rivers.

THE ENUMA ELISH

Much of Mesopotamian religion is in the form of epic poems – stories of the gods, what they do, and how they relate to each other and to humanity. The *Enuma Elish* is the Babylonian creation myth. Most think it dates from between the eighteenth and the sixteenth centuries BC, although there appear to be later editions of it, as recent as the seventh century BC. It begins:

When in the height heaven
  was not named,
And the earth beneath did not
  yet bear a name,
And the primeval Apsu,
  who begat them,
And chaos, Tiamut,
  the mother of them both
Their waters were mingled
  together,
And no field was formed,
  no marsh was to be seen;
When of the gods none had
  been called into being,
And none bore a name, and
  no destinies were ordained;
Then were created the gods
  in the midst of heaven...

THE EPIC OF GILGAMESH

Not all myths were directed towards ritual worship or festivals. The *Epic of Gilgamesh* is a free literary creation (originally carved into twelve clay tablets, some of which can be seen in the British Museum). It is the longest piece of Akkadian literature, and is well known in a number of editions across Mesopotamia. Gilgamesh was possibly a historical prince of Uruk (modern-day Iraq), and the epic is about his search for immortality. Overcome with grief at the death of his dear friend Enkidu, he resolves to learn how to conquer death. He has many adventures on his way to the wise Utnapishtim, who advises him to try to conquer Sleep, which is the younger brother of Death. Gilgamesh fails in this, and realizes that Death cannot be overcome and that man is mortal. The epic therefore is a very early account of humanity's search for immortality, failure in this search, and the inevitability of death for all. It also has an account of an extensive flood in it, much like the one in Genesis.

The epic reveals the Mesopotamian worldview – particularly the Babylonian view – that life is here and now, and what happens after death is ambiguous and unknown. Death is probably a place of dust and gloom: the dead should be buried well then, otherwise they will return to haunt the living. Offerings were made for the dead, in the hope that perhaps immortality could be achieved by ritually honouring their memory.

Egypt

GETTING READY FOR DEATH AND THE AFTERLIFE

In contrast to the ancient Mesopotamians' feelings of ambiguity towards death and the afterlife, the ancient Egyptians seemed to have a clear idea of what the afterlife had in store. Preparing for death and preserving the dead were developed into an artistic expression. To enhance the journey to the world of the dead, the Egyptians perfected mummification and the building of magnificent tombs – for that is what the pyramids are. These required sophisticated embalming techniques and impressive engineering feats. The myth of the dying and rising god was embodied in the god Osiris (following the rise and fall of the River Nile each year). Leading a good life on earth would influence the quality of life after death; spells and magic could continue to influence the lives of the deceased. The idea of divine kingship was well developed: all pharaohs were sons of the gods, and hence it was a priority to preserve the pharaoh's body to guarantee his ongoing well-being in the afterlife.

Akhenaten's Reforms: A Brief Experiment with Monotheism

For a short twenty-five years or so (1375–1350 BC), Pharaoh Amenophis IV gradually directed the Egyptians to the sole worship of the god Aten. It was an experiment in monotheism. Aten was the sun disk; he was the source of all life, and the pharaoh changed his own name to Akhenaten, which means "the one who is beneficial to Aten". The pharaoh himself acted as a sort of go-between, passing the life-giving power of Aten on to the people. The worship of Amun, the traditional supreme god and patron of the Pharaohs was suppressed. However, this reform did not last long and was resisted for what it was: a bizarre political manoeuvre by a king whose sanity was doubted. The reform was also unnecessary, as Egyptian gods were not in conflict with each other; they happily coexisted, and there is a wealth of stories and legends about them.

Right: A statuette for King Osorkon II (883–855 BC) depicting the family of the god Osiris. Osiris is flanked by Horus (left) and Isis (right).

The Gods of Egypt

Egypt was polytheistic; there were many gods, each with specific responsibilities and tasks. Each had to be appeased. Throughout Egypt's long history, some functions were carried out by more than one god.

God/goddess	Association
Amun	King of the gods; patron deity of the pharaohs; later identified with Ra, the sun god
Anubis	God of the dead; associated with tombs
Aten	The sun; for a short period he was the chief and only god
Hapi (Apis)	God of the Nile; a bull associated with fertility
Hathor	Goddess with a cow's head; goddess of the sky
Heqet	Goddess of birth and midwifery; recognized with a frog's head
Horus	Sun god
Isis	Goddess of the Nile; healer and protector of children
Khnum	God of the upper Nile; creator of gods, men, and water
Min	God of reproduction
Nut	Goddess of the sky
Osiris	God of crops and fertility
Ptah	God of the dead; also associated with creation and fertility
Re/Ra	Sun god; source of all life
Sebek	Water god; sometimes associated with evil and death
Sekhmet	Goddess with power over disease
Seth	God of storms and the desert; is violent and dangerous
Sunu	God of pestilence
Thoth	Moon god; god of learning and wisdom, and the inventor of writing
Uatchit	Protector of lower Egypt; has the head of a fly/cobra

Egyptian Religious Texts

Religion in Egypt was not written down in sophisticated and formal texts. It was more a loose collection of myths and stories. However, many were engraved on the walls of tombs and on and around coffins. These so-called "coffin texts" formed the main core of written religious materials. These eventually took form in the Middle Kingdom (c. 2050–1750 BC) as *The Book of the Dead* or, more precisely, *The Book of Going Forth by Day*. The book was to be laid with the dead in their coffin, and it instructed the deceased how to pass through into the afterlife.

A Speech by the Sun God Ra (Coffin Text no. 1130)

Hail in peace! I repeat to you the good deeds which my own heart did for me from within the serpent-coil, in order to silence strife...

I made the four winds, that every man might breathe in his time...

I made the great inundation, that the humble might benefit by it like the great...

I made every man like his fellow; and I did not command that they do wrong. It is their hearts which disobey what I have said...

I have created the gods from my sweat, and the people from the tears of my eye.

How Egypt Has Lasted So Long

Egypt is protected by natural boundaries: the desert in the west; the ocean in the north and east. Its source of fertility is the Nile river, which floods every year, and hence replenishes the land. Egypt is therefore dry (due to the desert) and fertile (due to the river), making it ideal both for the development of agriculture, cities, and human culture, and for the preservation of the same. Its history has been documented since around 3100 BC. The historian Manetho (323–245 BC), divided Egyptian history into thirty-one dynasties, and this naming system has become standard. These dynasties are gathered together in the Archaic period, then the Old, Middle, and New Kingdoms.

Greece and Rome

GRECO-ROMAN RELIGION

Greek and Roman religion often comes under one heading, as they became so intertwined during the Roman empire (first century BC–fifth century AD). The Romans used Greek culture as a unifying means for their empire: while the Latin of the Romans was the cultured language, Greek was the trade language. Religion was polytheistic. In some ways the gods were heightened humans: they loved and fought, did good and made mistakes. The myths of the gods were widely known. The gods of Rome and Greece were shared but had different names.

Greco-Roman religion has influenced many aspects of Western culture. In addition, it was the context in which Judaism and Christianity were born. Judaism actively embraced aspects of Greco-Roman culture, but firmly rejected the religious ethos. Christianity had to find a way of resisting, yet growing, within this religious mixture.

Athena, wearing crested helmet, bronze, c. 375 BC.

THE GREEK AND ROMAN GODS

Greek name	Roman name	Sphere of influence
Zeus	Jupiter	Chief god; ruler of the sky and weather; father of gods and men (but not creator). The gods lived on Mount Olympus, ruled by Zeus.
Aphrodite	Venus	Love, beauty, and fertility
Ares	Mars	War; a violent and quarrelsome god
Hermes	Mercury	Merchants and traders; messenger of the gods
Chronos	Saturn	Time and harvests
Artemis	Diana	Hunting, fertility, and childbirth
Athena	Minerva	War and handicrafts
Dionysus	Bacchus	Crops and fruit, wine; associated with the underworld
Hephaestus	Vulcan	Fire, volcanoes, and the blacksmith's forge; crafts
Hera	Juno	Marriage, women, and childbirth; also associated with the moon and is the wife of Zeus
Hestia	Vesta	Hearth and home, family; goddess of the city of Rome
Poseidon	Neptune	Earthquakes, the sea
Hades	Pluto	The underworld
Apollo	Sol	Flocks and herds, archery, music; associated with the sun/light, and medicine and healing
Demeter	Ceres	Corn and crops

Greek Religion

The central rite of Greek religion was sacrificing to the gods in order to appease them, win their favour, or simply offer thanks. This involved the slaughter of animals. Sacrifices were eaten. All of life was infused by religion, with one's duty to the gods inseparable from everyday life. The priests were often the city magistrates: there was little separation of civic and religious roles.

A category of demi-god also existed: these were the heroes, deified men, often associated with great deeds of a city or family clan. They were usually identified and deified after their deaths, and shrines were built to honour them. Achilles and Hercules are well-known heroes.

The Greeks had a love of wisdom – *philosophia* – that is, philosophy. Philosophical ideas overlapped with religion as well as emerging disciplines such as mathematics, logic, and governance. Pythagoras, Aristotle, Socrates, Plato, Heraclitus – these and many others have shaped global civilization and culture since, by asking (and answering) the "big questions": What is truth? What is real? How may I be significant? How can I know? How should I relate to the gods?

Roman Religion

While the Roman gods were similar to the Greek, Roman religious ideas were slightly different. They were concerned with *numina* – a spiritual guiding force that penetrated everything. The gods were like mysterious spirits who aroused reverential fear. The whole of civic life in Rome was geared towards ensuring the *numina* became (and remained) favourable towards humankind. For example, the month of March began with sacrifices to the god Mars for his blessing on the instruments of war: horses, arms, trumpets. Hence the civic and the religious were intermingled: civic virtue was related to public religious rites. A virtuous city governor's task was not only to ensure peace and public services were maintained, but also to ensure correct sacrifices to the gods were made at the right times.

Like the Greeks, the Romans had a broad range of myths and legends. Cities had temples at their heart, one noticeable example being the Greek temple to Artemis at Ephesus. Over the centuries, Roman emperors claimed to be divine. This was not unusual for the age, but the creed "Caesar is Lord" proved to be a defining testimony that distinguished "Roman" and "not-Roman".

IDEAS FROM GRECO-ROMAN RELIGION STILL IN USE TODAY

- **Cosmos:** The universe; this was an orderly, unified whole.

- **Holocaust:** A whole burnt offering of an animal to a god or the gods.

- **Hubris:** Over-the-top pride demonstrated by desiring to be equal to the gods, usually proving disastrous.

- **Logos:** Reason; the principle governing the cosmos. Christianity equates *logos* (as "Word") with Jesus Christ.

- **Mysteria:** Mysteries, or the Mystery Religions of Isis, Eleusis, and Mithras. Revelation of the mysteries was given only through dramatic initiation rites.

- **Mythos:** A story, and in particular a defining and authoritative story about the gods.

- **Numen:** Spirit, usually associated with a place, such as a stream, woodland, mountain, or sacred place; a sacred force.

- **Philosophia:** Literally, the love of wisdom. A system of ideas equipping people to cope with life; for example, Stoicism and Neo-Platonism.

- **Religio:** That which binds us to the gods; religion.

- **Theos:** A deity; God as supreme being.

One of the great wonders of the ancient world, the Temple of Artemis, was located in Ephesus (modern-day Turkey). It underwent various phases of destruction and rebuilding, and today only foundational fragments remain (right). The wealth and grand scale of the temple in the artist's impression, above, show the significance of Artemis-worship for the Ephesians.

Northern Europe

THE CELTS AND THE GERMANIC TRIBES

Modern European life and thought can be traced back to the "old gods" of northern Europe. There are two traditions identified: the Celts (now recognized particularly in Ireland, Scotland, Wales, parts of south-western England and north-western France) and the Germanic tribes (particularly the Scandinavians and the Vikings). There is a rejuvenation of these traditions today, with the Druids of Britain, Celtic worship themes in modern Christianity, and the New Age movement drawing on the rites, rituals, and symbols of both traditions. Like Greco-Roman traditions, much has made it into the worldview and language of Europeans, from Christmas traditions to names of the days of the week.

The Importance of Myth

The first people to record the myths and stories were mainly Roman, so no doubt some bias has crept into the retellings we have today. Also, early Christian missionaries who spread out over Europe recorded various myths and folk tales. Much of this is interpreted through the lens of early European Christianity. For example, many of the Scandinavian myths were written down by one Snorri Sturluson (d. 1264) in Iceland. Many of the stories were oral traditions, and hence reinterpreted in the telling by either Roman or Christian storytellers: their religious aspects may well have come unstuck from their broader cultural functions (such as entertainment, explanation, or celebration). Both Celtic and Germanic traditions are polytheistic – there were many gods.

Celtic Religion

There has been some reinterpretation of pre-Roman Celts (Gauls) by the Romans, but it is clear that the Celts had a horned god called Cernunnos. He may have been represented by a stag, and was probably related to fertility and war. The Horned One sometimes had a consort. This Earth Mother was worshipped, and there are many Irish stories about her mystery, vigour, and beauty. Water played a role in Celtic religion, particularly springs, wells, caves, and sacred groves. Human sacrifice is evident, and there was probably a "cult of the head" – the human head is a major theme in Celtic art. Celts believed in an afterlife, and Druids performed sacrifice, divination, and a liturgy.

Germanic Religion and the Vikings

Again, coming to us through Roman interpretations, the Germanic tribes (such as the Goths) were warlike, and hence Roman observers assumed a war god was dominant. There is a prominent female deity, probably associated with fertility: women were associated with holiness, purity, and prophecy. Divination, often associated with horses, was common. The Norse gods – those of the northern Scandinavians and Vikings – are widely known: Woden (Odin), Twiz, Thor, Frey, and their homeland Valhalla are still studied today.

Silver Gundestrup cauldron bowl, a Celtic ritual vessel of the 2nd century BC. Inside, on the left, is Cernunnos, king of the animals.

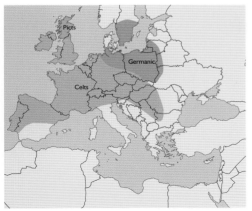

The Vanir Deities of Norse Mythology

These are the "lesser" gods of Norse mythology, which are largely associated with maintenance and reproduction.

- **Njord**: The deity who controls wind and sea.

- **Frey**: Son of Njord, deity of rain and sun, he is also associated with fertility. The English Friday is named after Frey.

- **Freyja (Frigg)**: Consort of Odin and sister of Frey, she is goddess of love and fertility.

- **Heimdall**: Watchman of the gods.

The Aesir Deities of Norse Mythology

The Aesir deities were the "active" gods of Norse legend, the victors in a series of mythological battles that pitted them against the Vanir deities. After the war was finished, and the deities united, the Aesir nevertheless retained their associations with war.

- **Woden (Odin)**: Named Woden in the south, and Odin in the north (among the Norse peoples), he was father of all the gods, the god of war, who was worshipped particularly by warriors and tribal leaders. The English Wednesday (literally "Woden's day") is named after him.

- **Thor**: Along with Odin, Thor is the best-known deity. He is the god of thunder, and is depicted with a large hammer. He is the strongest of the gods, and also the god of fertility (and hence "Thor's day" – Thursday).

- **Balder**: Son of Odin and Freyja, he is a god of beauty and brightness.

- **Loki**: A mischievous deity, he is the father of monsters.

Viking memorial picture stone of Sanda Gotland showing the saga of Thor, son of Odin. It dates from the 10th century AD.

21

Indus Valley Civilization

HARAPPANS AND ARYANS

The Harappan civilization (3300–1300 BC) was located in the Indus Valley region, what is now Pakistan. Excavations in Harappa and Mohenjo-daro since 1922 have indicated a rich and diverse culture. Like the Nile river in Egypt, the Indus was vital for the development of a strong agricultural economy and sophisticated city life. The Harappan civilization fell to the Aryans who invaded from their homelands in Mesopotamia in the middle of the second millennium BC. This overlaying of Aryan on Harappan culture meant a mixing of religious beliefs and practices. The emerging Vedic religion, built on the Veda texts, became known as Brahmanism, which became the dominant worldview of the south Asian subcontinent. Brahmanism is the root of Hinduism today.

Below: A view of the Indus valley. The Harappans were able to sustain a sophisticated civilization because of the valley's regular and wide flowing river, the Indus, which was fed by the winter snows of the Himalayas and the Asian monsoon.
Top right: The spring festival of Holi celebrates the love of Krishna and Radha. It begins with a bonfire which the Vedic scriptures teach destroys demonic forces.
Right: A Vietnamese dancing Shiva. Shiva is thought to be sourced from the religion of the Indus Valley civilization.

The Harappan Religion

With life dominated by the Indus river, religion was related to natural cycles of fertility. Water was associated with ritual washing and purity; ancient temple-cities reveal extensive baths. Life itself was dependent upon the river, and hence the river was sacred. Highly developed drainage and sewerage systems on a grid structure suggest the priority of ritual cleanliness and the importance of water.

The intermeshing of civic and religious would have been the norm – perhaps there was even a "sacred kingship". There is also evidence to suggest that the later Hindu gods derived from the Harappan ones. Excavations have unearthed female images with oversized breasts, suggestive of fertility goddesses and even a matriarchal society. An image of a sitting god with an erect phallus (perhaps a yogi in contemplation) could be an early embodiment of the Hindu god Shiva. This, with the goddesses, can be likened to Shiva and his consort Shakti. Other male images of the Harappan civilization are three-faced with horns, much like the *trimurti* of the three Hindu gods Brahma, Vishnu, and Shiva.

The Aryan "Invasion"
● ●

Rather than ousting the Harappan civilization forcefully, the Aryans probably simply merged into it over 500 or so years. The Harappans had declined, possibly due to deforestation, and were largely vulnerable. The Aryans were probably nomadic, or at least certainly comfortable with livestock and migration: the Harappans were pushed east and south, and now their descendants populate southern India. The Aryans brought their literature with them, which we know today as the Vedas – the oldest recognized scriptures of Hinduism. In fact "Vedism", or "Vedic religion" is a category within Hinduism, signifying a strong literature-based religious practice, and it is largely conservative, upholding the Hindu hierarchical caste system based on the four divisions of the cosmic man, *purusha*.

FIRE AND WATER

The deities of the Vedas were manifestations of nature: Indra, the deity of lightning and war, was the main god. Agni, god of fire, is still worshipped today. Fire and water are dominant images in Hinduism. Vedic religion was dominated by ritual: fire and the horse sacrifice associated with kingship were known. Fire links earth with heaven, and humanity with *devas*, spirit beings. It transforms the worldly and divine realms. Hence, fire, water, sacrifice, and fertility, along with features like *soma* (a hallucinogenic), formed the elements of the Harappan and Aryan religions. This in time spread eastward into modern India, and it is from this that the Brahaminic, then Hindu tradition arose. The priests of the Vedic literature were Brahmins, the top of the Hindu caste system, and they communicated this growing ideology to the rest of the people. As priests they controlled the fire rituals; they also advised the kings and controlled kingly succession.

DHARMA AND *KARMA*

By the 700s BC, it was widely believed that the gods could be influenced through correct ritual and sacrifice. The Vedas also introduce the ideas of *dharma* (duty, morality) and *karma* (action/fate). These are both played out in *samsara*, the cycle of birth, death, and rebirth. The Sanskrit language developed during this time, which led to more works of religious literature. Thus the foundations were laid for much of modern Hinduism – indeed, much of the religious and cultural air that southern Asia breathes today.

African Religion

DIVERSITY AND COMMUNITY

African religion is as diverse as the land itself. Many aspects of African religion were influenced by Christianity during the colonial era (nineteenth and early twentieth centuries), and Islam before that. During the Atlantic slave trade in the sixteenth to the nineteenth centuries, the African slaves took their religious beliefs with them to the New World. As Africa found a stronger voice in the twentieth century after colonialism, its religions are being rejuvenated. Common themes of primal religions have emerged: fertility and kingship are related in that a kingdom needs a strong agricultural base, and therefore the king is responsible for fertility. He becomes both earthly and divine, or at least priestly, in ensuring the appropriate rituals and sacrifices are carried out.

BEING HUMAN

A person isn't such until named. Infanticide is not regarded as wrong until the child is given a name, and hence a personality, often in honour of an ancestor. The "new human" then inherits the ancestor's nature, qualities, and future status. If one is not part of a community, one is less than human. Being thrown out of the village is a life-threatening banishment.

GODS AND SPIRITS

African religions are largely polytheistic. While many tribes do acknowledge one Supreme Being, he is remote. God's power is experienced as refracted, like a light through a prism, by and through local deities. Local religions are mediated by priests, prophets, diviners, and healers. Healing is a major activity: sickness is seen as a way the gods communicate with people. A cured person may act as a mouthpiece of the god.

The Importance of Community

African religion is generally passed down orally, rather than through a body of religious texts. Hence the authority of the ancestors is important. Fertility is therefore also important: how can I become an ancestor and pass down the stories unless I marry and have children? Thus symbolic art is common: masks, body painting, body piercing, small models, and sculptures all have a role in endorsing and passing on the tribe's religious stories. They embody the story.

Religious expression is in the community. One participates in the community and in religious festivals and rites by being initiated into it at the appropriate age (usually puberty). Coming-of-age rites – circumcision, and in some cultures, clitorisectomy – are followed by marriage, and the expectation of children: all this to continue the community. It includes the ancestors, usually back to the third or fourth generation. They are active and largely benevolent and must be consulted in community decisions: they are part of the whole religious worldview. A community is thus defined by those who tell the same story.

A wooden Yoruba shrine figure in the form of mother and child. At the base is a fertility scene. Originating from Nigeria in the 19th–20th century.

The gods and spirits are thought of in human categories. Religion tends to deal with day-to-day issues, hence is "this-worldly". Creation myths usually talk of original order, but in the creative process this order has become disturbed, most notably through death. The physical features of the land have spiritual qualities and power. They are the gods, and behave in human ways. Experience of these deities is important: one can know their will in dreams.

If themes of death and the threat of disorder dominate, then funerals and mourning must be done correctly. This new ancestor may now well become a guardian spirit: the dead are to be treated with respect. Overall, to ensure the welfare of the community (which includes the ancestors), human actions must promote harmony, and be discreet and orderly.

A "Portable" Religion

Many African tribes are nomadic, or at least mobile to some degree, and so religion must be portable. There are few big, permanent temples. Local improvised shrines are the norm. They can be decorated landscape features that have taken on significance because of their place in a story or because an important event happened there, like a healing. Because of the need for portability, the shrines are sometimes quite small, like the nineteenth-century Nigerian example of an *ikegobo* shrine below. They might also be associated with sacrifice. Storytelling is elevated to a ritual and artistic form, accompanied by dance and music, which transmit the religious stories.

In central Mali, wooden figures have been carved to resemble the religious figure, Hogon, in his clan house, which acts to protect the Dogon ethnic group's ancestors.

The Reason for Death

Many of the African stories are about death and the threat of disorder. One common myth is that of the Supreme Being sending eternal life by a slow-moving animal, like the chameleon. However, because he is so slow, the Supreme Being sends a faster messenger – a lizard (or a hare) – to inform humans about death. The faster animal beats the chameleon with the news, and hence humans are subject to death.

Ritual
● ●

Religious ritual is pre-eminently sacrifice. The blood of a sheep, goat, cattle or chicken – representing the life force – wards off evil. It is a means of communication between humans and the gods. Festivals of the seasons, coronations, healing rituals – these and others are found throughout Africa. Sacred music, believed to be received from the deities, is common.

Shamanism

RELIGION OF ECSTASY

While mainly associated with Siberia (particularly the Tungus of eastern Siberia) and northern and central Asia, Shamanism nevertheless is found in many other cultures. Korean, Mongolian, Native American, Tibetan, some African, and some South American religions have shamanistic elements. Shamanism has ancient roots: it is one of the oldest known expressions of religious belief, with cave paintings in Europe depicting shamans travelling with animals and spirits. These paintings have been dated at around 30000 BC.

The Centrality of the Shaman

The shaman has often been misunderstood to be a "witch doctor" or "medicine man". Although often operating as a healer, the shaman is much more than this for he or she is a seer – they see into another realm of existence.

A shaman is in fact a prophetic or priestly person, who holds the position due to spiritual charisma, a calling by vision or dream, or through heredity. They act as an intermediary between this world and the other. They are specialists but yet may have a "normal job" or role in the community when that of shaman is not required. Shamans probably had to undertake a severe initiation task, including miraculously recovering from a major illness.

The shaman is often assisted by the totem animal of the tribe. The animal may be their progenitor, that is, the animal from which the tribe is believed to be descended. The wolf and eagle are common totem animals for north Asian shamanism. The characteristics of the animal – power, wisdom, fertility, cunning, strength, and speed – are imbibed by the shaman: the totem animal assists him.

Shamans are often the gatekeepers for a tribe, holding the tribe's legends. They may be called in for guidance; for example, they can direct where to fish and hunt.

ECSTASY AND TRANCE

The shaman's message is attained by entering a trance, often with the aid of sophisticated and lengthy rituals and so achieving a state of heightened spiritual ecstasy is important. This may be assisted by drugs, blood constriction, and rhythmic drumming. In some cultures, the spirits are said to enter and possess the shaman.

While in a trance the shaman travels on a spiritual journey to the other world to gain messages, healing balms, or instructions from spirit beings – a journey that may involve a ritual or trance-like death and resurrection. The shaman returns with these messages, and while still in a trance speaks them; these are then translated by trained assistants. The shaman is unlikely to remember anything after the event.

Shamans, such as these Siberian Tuvans, usually undertake their craft in colourful clothing, adorned with fur or feathers of the tribe's totem animal.

● SEE ALSO

PRIMAL RELIGION PP. 12–13   BUDDHISM PP. 50–51
NATIVE AMERICAN RELIGION PP. 30–31   NEW AGE MOVEMENT PP. 118–119
THE PEOPLES OF THE ANDES PP. 32–33

Tibetan Buddhism is a mixture of the ancient shamanistic religion of Tibet, called Bön, and Buddhism originally from India. The Tibetan community in exile in India has a State Oracle – a shaman – called the Nechung Oracle. It was with his advice and assistance that the Dalai Lama made a safe passage out of Tibet in 1959. This scene shows a Tibetan–Buddhist ceremony at the Nechung Monastery, India.

A Threefold Universe

In shamanism there is an upper world, a middle world (here and now), and an underworld. This threefold universe is held together by an axis mundi, a feature that penetrates the centre of all three, such as a significant mountain or a large tree. Physical features of the land join the three levels of existence; for example, wells, springs, and caves are channels from the underworld to this world. Mountains are pathways between this and the upper world. In fact a variety of objects that reach skywards can be a significant connector between this and the upper world: trees, tall buildings, summits, and telegraph poles are all used. People will also build cairns – artificial mountains – as connectors between the realms. Cairns on mountain passes and summits enhance and heighten the natural elevation. These act as conduits, or symbolic and ritual pathways on which the shaman can travel.

Mongols and Tenger

The Mongol khans (thirteenth century AD) were shamanists. They believed in a personified sky, which they named Tenger. Tenger oversaw their destiny, and gave Genghis Khan his mandate to conquer the world. Everything nomads on the central Asian steppe did was under the care of Munkh Tenger, the eternal sky. Shamans were called upon to undertake spiritual journeys to Tenger and inform the Mongols of his will. In Mongolia today, religion is a mix of tengerism and Buddhism: Buddhist prayer flags adorn shamanic cairns, called obo. For the Mongols, the horse, the wolf, and the doe are totemic: rituals continue today to the spirit of Genghis Khan, which is embodied in his nine horsetail banner.

Shamanism in the West

Shamanism made a comeback in the 1960s, particularly in its North American guise through the drug culture of that decade and the writings of Carlos Castañeda. In 1968, he published *The Teachings of Don Juan* in which he describes his training in shamanism by his tutor, the "man of knowledge" Don Juan Matus of the Yaqui people who live in Mexico and Arizona. The book immediately attained cult status.

Today, shamanism is a significant strand of New Age belief and practice, because of its spiritual journey motif, the desire for wholeness and healing, the experience of meditation and trance, and the opportunities for either sex to exercise these powers. In addition, the New Age tends to see the older as more authentic, and so many are attracted to shamanism because of its antiquity.

Pacifica and Australian Aboriginal

MELANESIAN, MICRONESIAN, AND POLYNESIAN

The South Pacific has two broadly different religious traditions. One is that of the peoples of the Pacific islands: this includes the Melanesian, Micronesian, and Polynesian groups. While now strongly influenced by Christianity in many of the island archipelagos, just under the surface there is nevertheless a lively primal religious culture.

The other major religious tradition is that of the Aboriginal peoples of Australia. Their religious worldview is unique, and in many ways quite different from that of their Pacific neighbours. It is considered to be one of the oldest religions. To the untrained eye, it looks "primitive"; however, Aboriginal religion is as sophisticated as any other.

The Islands of Pacifica

Due to migration patterns over the last one thousand or so years, the worldview and religious practices of the various Pacific nations have much in common. The ocean is huge, and the islands are small and rich in vegetation. Hence ocean navigation, distance, migration, and dense vegetation have all informed religious beliefs of the Pacific.

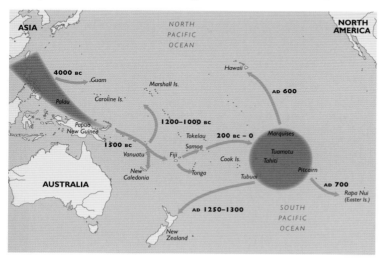

Map shows the migration patterns of Pacifica.

Top right: A Papua New Guinean man in ritual dress. Totem animals of the Pacific are often birds. This man has dressed himself in imitation of one of the thousands of species of birds in Papua New Guinea.

Religious Beliefs

There is a distinction between the physical and spiritual worlds, yet they are intertwined. Spirits permeate everything – there is an essential animism to Pacific religion. Festivals entail dressing up to look like the spirits of the land; for example, people will adorn themselves with bird feathers. As in shamanism, the idea of totem animals is prevalent.

Pacific religion is dominated by myth and ritual, with creation and hero myths. Genealogy is prioritized: it honours the achievements of the ancestors who have travelled vast distances and gives identity to the living. Some of the ancestors, particularly those who fathered the tribe, are partly deified. The deities themselves are often part human. Maui (a mythic demigod), for example, fished up the North Island of New Zealand from his canoe (the South Island). Land and place are sacred. For example, in Maori, the word *whenua* means both "land" and "placenta": the land nourishes, as a placenta nourishes a foetus. Hence both are sacred because they give life.

THE STATUS OF WOMEN

Humans pre-exist in the other world and travel to this one. Women are therefore honoured as the bringers of humans to this world. They often have an elevated status in rituals, rites, and community protocols. The spirits of the deceased depart over the ocean to the original mythical homeland, Hawaiki (variously named).

The Australian Landmass

In contrast to the Pacific islands, the Australian landmass is huge, hot, and dry with little rainfall and few rivers. The worldview of the Australian Aboriginals is shaped largely by the vastness of the landscape: this landscape is populated with unique animals that look and move in ways not known anywhere else. Whereas the ancestors of the Pacific navigated over vast oceans, the Aboriginal ancestors "navigate" over vast land distances.

THE DREAMTIME

The Dreamtime and totemism are prevalent in the religious beliefs of the Aboriginal peoples. The Dreamtime was the period long ago when the deities walked on the earth and gave shape to the land, animals, humans, and their societies. Because of the harsh environment, both humans and animals must be ingenious to survive. Animals in Australia look and act uniquely – kangaroos bounce, lizards sprint, and cockatoos don extravagant headcrests – and so must humans. Such hopping, bounding, and flamboyancy characterizes Aboriginal rituals. The dream lines that cross the landscape are the spiritual tracks that guide people in their hunting; the Dreamtime is alive in the present.

The Aboriginals therefore have an "eco-psychism" – they relate to the land in spiritual ways often misunderstood by the now dominant post-colonial descendants who share Australia with them. The spirits of the Dreamtime link the Aboriginals to their clans: fertility rites are important, and some creation myths are dominated by fertility, copulation, and eternal pregnancy stories. Not only are children needed in this harsh environment to

Uluru (Ayers Rock), Uluru National Park, Australia. The Anangu people of central Australia associate Uluru with their creation stories.

populate the land of the Dreamtime, but they are also required to carry on the rituals so that the land will be prosperous and the spirits favourable, particularly the spirits of the animals.

Australia itself then is imagined by the spiritual eye of the Aboriginal as a sacred place criss-crossed by dream lines. These are well known among the various moving tribes, so as to form a single united place. Spirits of the Dreamtime have infused this land, giving meaning to the features that are sacred, and each has its story.

POLYNESIAN *TAPU* AND *MANA*

The Polynesian idea of *tapu* means something being forbidden or dangerous. The English word "taboo" comes from this. *Tapu* is nuanced with holiness and purity. *Mana* is power: this could be the power residing in the landscape feature due to its place in a myth, or it could refer to charismatic power or honour that resides in a chief. *Mana* can be given, taken, and destroyed. *Tapu* as well can be abused and dishonoured. A person with high *mana* can lift the *tapu* (the sacredness and forbiddenness) and make something common and accessible again, as with an area defiled by death or bad spirits.

The *mana* of a great chief is depicted in an ornately carved pole by New Zealand Maori.

Native American Religion

NATURAL AND SPIRITUAL WORLDS

Native North American religious traditions are extremely varied. Getting a good understanding of them is a challenge because of the Native Americans' long history of oppression. Colonization of the land often led to their forced conversion to Christianity, and government policy pushed many Native Americans into reservations. Nevertheless, now in a post-colonial era, first nation stories are having a fairer hearing. There is growing recognition of their rich and colourful culture and religion. This, together with New Age devotees mining Native American traditions for symbols, myths, and spiritual techniques, has resulted in Native American religion gaining some new momentum.

A Canadian Inuit elder. Without the seal, the Inuit's livelihood would be very precarious. Inuit shamans will call on the sea goddess Takanaluk to "release" the seal for the hunt.

The Importance of Nature

Native Americans are intimately allied with the natural world. Like Australian Aboriginal beliefs, the land itself is sacred and has supernatural meaning. Certain animals – totems – embody spiritual significance, such as the wolf, eagle, buffalo, cougar, alligator, and coyote. A spirit of thankfulness pervades Native American religion: apologies were made to the spirit of the tree or the buffalo when it was cut or killed.

God, the One Great Spirit

Creation myths explain how animals and humans came into being. The Pawnee's Great Spirit Tirawahat created the cosmos. The world of the Iroquois was created by twins – one good, one an evil trickster. In some tribes, creation myths are related directly to the animals on which the tribe relies. For example, the Inuit of northern Canada believe in the underwater goddess Takanaluk: she "releases" the seals to be hunted, if the Inuit have kept the taboos. The creation of the seal is less important than its availability to be hunted. The cosmos is ordered and hierarchical, but mythical figures – for example the trickster twin of a creation myth – often reflect the disorder of human nature.

A totem pole located in Stanley Park, Vancouver, Canada. The dominant eagle image represents intelligence and resourcefulness.

Rituals and Ceremonies

At heart, Native American cultures are shamanistic. The shaman is the link between this and the other world. More generally, humans themselves mediate between spirits and nature. The harmony of the cosmos – the relationship between physical nature here and now, and the spirit world – is determined by humans. Some common elements of rituals include:

- Rhythm: use of drum and dance, chanting and singing.

- Natural cycles: celebrations of solstice and equinox, planting and harvesting, rituals before and after the hunt.

- Initiations: rituals associated with first steps, puberty, and marriage.

- Taboos: success in life (particularly hunting and warfare) was about avoiding the taboos (avoiding doing wrong, and appeasing the spirits accordingly).

- Spirits: relating to a unique guardian spirit who supports life.

An injured warrior at the
Battle of Wounded Knee.

Native American Indians dancing at a
Fiesta parade.

WARRIORS

A culture of warriorship is common throughout the world. It implies an afterlife: to die well is to gain a better afterlife. Life here and now is the place to be tested in readiness for the afterlife. Heroism gains your place in tribal lore. Invincibility in battle is sought: the Sioux warrior Black Elk wore his "ghost shirt" into battle at Wounded Knee (1890). He recalled: "All the time the bullets were buzzing around me and I was not hurt. I was not even afraid. It was like being in a dream about shooting."

The idea of a "ghost shirt" implies being strengthened or protected by an ancestral ghost; belief that the dead can come back as ghosts is common. Some tribes have a more explicit belief in a type of reincarnation, while all believe in some sort of afterworld.

SHAPES AND NUMBERS

The Native American religious worldview can be understood by the use of shapes. These shapes mesh with each other, signifying wholeness and oneness. Certain numbers are also understood to have special significance.

■ The circle encompasses all of the cosmos: at its centre is the Great Spirit.

■ The circle is divided by a wavy line. There are opposites (male/female, light/dark) but they are not in opposition. Complements are valued.

■ The triangle represents an ethic of "give and take", its corners symbolizing human need, spiritual power, and ceremonial action. For the Mohawk, if the crops fail (human need), then the rain dance is done (ceremonial action) and the thunder god sends rain (spiritual power).

■ The number "4" is sacred: for example, there are four seasons, four directions, four elements (earth, air, water, fire), four virtues (generosity, courage, respect, wisdom).

■ The number "7" is significant across many cultures: among the Native Americans it might represent the number of significant ancestors (the Ojibwa people), or the number of important rites (the Lakota people).

THE SWEAT LODGE CEREMONY

Many religious traditions are concerned with purification, spiritual renewal, healing, and rebirth. The North American plains tribes (Blackfoot, Cheyenne, Apache, and others) used to build temporary "sweat lodges" as places where these ideals could be experienced. Willows were bent to build a framework, much like a self-supporting tent today, and it was covered with skins. The resulting dome shape represented the cosmos. Water was poured on hot rocks inside, and a person entered and, in effect, had a sauna. The lodge was sometimes half-buried, emphasizing the connection to Mother Earth. When used as an initiation, it brought the person closer to the One Great Spirit of the tribe. Here, three Native American men pose outside a Crow village sweat lodge in Montana.

The Peoples of the Andes

THE INCAS

The Andes mountain range is the longest unbroken mountain chain in the world, located on the western side of South America. The terrain of this region varies from flat plains to tall mountains and high plateaus. Before the Spanish conquest in the sixteenth century, the Inca empire was dominant. The main ethnic group now is the Quecha, numbering around 11 million, and spread across Peru, Ecuador, Bolivia, Chile, Colombia, and Argentina. Another populous group is the Aymara (approximately 2 million) who occupy the *alteplano* – the high plain over 12,000 feet.

Andean Religion

Andean religion has many things in common with other primal religions: the desire for harmony between humans, nature, and gods; rituals related to crops and livelihood; initiation ceremonies; rituals of fertility for animals and humans; and spirits associated with landforms. A priest or shaman figure called a *paqo* is involved with divination and healing.

The height of the Inca empire lasted from the mid-1400s to the mid-1500s. The Inca worldview was twofold: Father Sun (Viracocha) and the moon goddess together regulated time and seasons, while the emperor held together the heavens and human affairs. Human sacrifice was probably carried out in temples. Cuzco, the capital, was believed to be the navel of the world; the Inca (that is, the emperor) who lived there was expected to facilitate fertility and success. The Sun God temple at its centre was somehow linked to the Milky Way, which the Inca believed to be a heavenly river.

In the 1530s the Spanish invaded and conquered the empire. But it was not only superior weapons and technology that led to the downfall of the Incas; the rapid spread of smallpox and other highly contagious diseases ultimately sealed their fate as a lost empire of antiquity.

Worship of the sun god was at the centre of Incan religious practice. They crafted many images of the sun using the precious metals that made the empire rich, namely gold, such as this Peruvian relic.

Ancestors and Spirits

Incan society was dominated by their relationship to divine ancestors and *huacas*, spirits of the mountains. The highest mountains were home to the *apus*, which were more powerful local deities. These local deities were responsible for the sending of thunder, hail, rain, wind, and fire. They were embodied in landforms: rocks, springs, and rivers. They were recognized and acknowledged by various offerings.

PACHAMAMA

However, Pachamama, the Earth Mother, was the chief focus of all Incan and even modern religious expression. After the Spanish conquest, Pachamama merged with the Virgin Mary, and much religion today is a mixture of indigenous and Catholic elements. Nevertheless, Pachamama's influence cannot be underestimated. Pachamama is motherly, close, and accessible. This is in contrast to the deities of other primal religions in which the chief deity is often male and usually remote. As Earth Mother, Pachamama is the sustainer of all life: she is alive and provides food for all. The mother idea is strong: Pachamama is a nurturing mother, offering life, nourishment, and security. Living things are not just created by her; they actually are her.

In the month of August, which is early spring in the southern hemisphere, the agricultural season begins. Pachamama is awakened and ready to receive seed. Ceremonies are performed to favour her and produce good harvests. Coca and food are given as burnt offerings, and sometimes a llama's foetus, mixed with animal fat and coca, are offered. Drink offerings, particularly the local alcohol *chichi*, is poured out on the ground to thank and sustain Pachamama.

● SEE ALSO
SHAMANISM PP. 26–27
NEW AGE MOVEMENT AND
ESOTERICA PP. 118–119

The Significance of the Jaguar

The Inca (and today's Quecha) honoured the jaguar as the totem animal. Essentially Quecha religion is shamanism: there is a need to connect the three layers of the cosmos – the lower, this layer, and the upper – and the shaman with his or her totem animal is able to do this. The jaguar is a good swimmer, and hence can descend to the lower realms (the underwater realm). A good climber, it can also ascend to the higher realm. The jaguar is not only the shaman's inspiration for the spiritual journey, but also the shaman's alter ego and competitor: it can travel faster and farther than the shaman. It is a spiritual creature, occupying a role of mystery in Quecha society.

The Earth Mother is depicted with arms outstretched, sun and moon on her breasts, and, in some images, with a baby about to be born. Other representations often associate her with a circle of light and dark, implying that she is the source of all life and sustenance. Pachamama has influenced the New Age movement, finding expression in Mother Earth, the mother goddess, and Gaia beliefs and rituals.

MACHU PICCHU

Machu Picchu in the mountains of southern Peru is perhaps the best-known temple city of the Incas. Located at 7,900 feet, it was probably a private estate of the emperor, but much of its religious function seems to have been to do with the worship of the sun. It was probably situated in relation to certain astronomical features as well, implying a sacred geography.

THE COCA LEAF

Coca leaf is chewed incessantly by the Quecha, and in its natural form is a mild stimulant to overcome fatigue, hunger, thirst, and altitude sickness. It is also mildly anaesthetic, it constricts blood vessels (it's good for nose bleeds at altitude), and because of its high calcium levels, it's good for bone injuries. In religious rituals, it is used as offerings to *apus*, the sun, and Pachamama. A shaman will chew the leaf before invoking a trance, and it is also used in divination. Not surprisingly, coca is the natural source for the drug cocaine.

Hinduism

A WAY OF LIFE

Hinduism is an umbrella term that covers a vast number of beliefs and rituals. It is rooted in the ancient Vedas, scriptures that are several thousand years old. Hinduism has grown to be a way of life for more than 800 million people. It is chiefly nurtured in the soil of India, although it has also followed the immigration of Indian peoples around the world. For example, Trinidad (in the Caribbean) and Bali (in Indonesia) are both influenced by Hinduism. Many of the key ideas in Hinduism influence other religions in both Asia and the West.

Hinduism has no one historical founder (although there are many influential thinkers and reformers), and has no unified belief system (although there is a loose collection of beliefs common to all). For example, Hindus differ in their beliefs about what's wrong with the world and what needs to happen to resolve it. There is no one centralized authority or institutional structure (like standardized scriptures, a "church", or a pope). There is no one religious language (although the main texts are in Sanskrit). Hinduism has no central place of significance (although many places of pilgrimage).

It may be best understood as an evolving religious culture, or a way of life: it is a spiritual and intellectual quest that allows a search for the sacred to happen in many different ways.

Hindu Gods

At the popular level, Hinduism appears to be polytheistic: people worship many gods through many paths (*marga*), disciplines (*yoga*), and philosophies (*dharshana*).

Three gods (the *trimurti*) are given priority: Brahma (the creator), Vishnu (the sustainer), and Shiva (the destroyer). Each has a female consort (Saraswati, Lakshmi, and Parvati, respectively). There are also many other gods appearing as kings, ascetics, dancers, and animals. An *avatar* is an appearance of a god on earth.

A Hindu may give their devotion to one deity or many. For example, someone who worships Vishnu is called a Vaishnavite. Someone who worships Shiva is a Shaivite. Various new sects have arisen over time, as have devotional reforms. Devotional sects (*bhakti*) arose throughout India from the sixth century AD. These sects freed people

A depiction of the *trimurti*: Brahma; Vishnu; and Shiva.

from the dry rituals and strict rules of the Vedic religion, and offered the worshipper union with god. *Bhakti-marga* (the way of devotion) could be considered to be an in-between form of Hindu practice that combines the rich teachings of the Vedic texts with the desire for personal devotion to one god. Devotional expressions of Hinduism have generated many stories, songs, and poems, as well as enriching many of the languages of India.

Hindu Worship

A Hindu may actually worship many gods (polytheism), or only one god (monotheism), or a Hindu may understand all reality to be one (monism). Hence popular religious acts may be as diverse as visiting temples and doing *puja* (acts of worship), adoring images, going on pilgrimages, reading and listening to holy texts, worshipping at sites such as rivers, summits, and passes, and honouring objects in which spirits may dwell or which represent aspects of monism. For example, Mount Kailash in western Tibet is revered by Shaivites as the abode of the god Shiva.

Modern Hinduism in India

In the last days of British colonial rule in India (which ended in 1948), various Hindu reforms emerged that have shaped India's nationalism. Aurobindo, Tilak, Ramakrishna, and Gandhi were early reformers, followed by Ram Mohan Roy, Dayananda Saraswati, and Vivekananda. All tried to adapt Hinduism for modern times, either through pragmatic changes needed after the British left and the modern state of India was born, or a call to return to the ancient traditions of Vedism. Several reformers challenged polytheism, along with idol and *yoni-lingam* veneration. Others challenged the foundational notions of *karma* and reincarnation, saying these ideas blocked social reform. Yet others promoted the unity of all religions.

The *yoni-lingam* is a very common Hindu object of veneration, representing the unity of life, the union of Shiva and his consort Parvati, and therefore fertility. It is a very common sight in India today to see people by the roadside placing garlands on *yoni-lingam* as acts of devotion to the god Shiva, often with prayers for conception and the safe birth of children.

AVATARS OF VISHNU

Vishnu is the Hindu god that is most recognizable as *avatar* – god on earth. He takes many forms, including:

- the fish (*matsya*)

- the tortoise (*kurma*)

- the boar (*varaha*)

- the man-lion (*narasimha*)

- the dwarf (*vamana*)

- Rama with the axe (*parasurama*)

- Rama, the hero of the *Ramayana* epic

- Krishna, the god who counsels Arjun about his caste duty in the *Bhagavad Gita* text

- Buddha

- Kalkin, the final *avatar* of Vishnu who is yet to appear on a white horse to judge the world and herald in a new age

A statue of Krishna.

Hinduism

LITERATURE OF THE HINDUS

No one body of sacred texts is common to all Hindus. Roughly, there are six groups of texts, which developed over time and in different historical contexts. Hindu texts can be divided into two major groups: *sruti* are the texts that are revealed or "heard"; *smriti* are the texts that are remembered. Some regard the *sruti* texts to be more authoritative for doctrine and ritual, because they were "heard" from God.

Sruti texts

These texts are believed to be rooted in divine revelation.

THE VEDAS

There are four groups of Vedas: the *Rig*, *Yajur*, *Sama*, and *Atharva*, all dating 1500–1200 BC. Myth and ritual dominate the Vedas. They celebrate the gods of earth (Aditi), sky (Varuna, Indra, Surya), and fire (Agni). Much of Vedic religion today is ritual associated with fire, and is influenced by these texts.

THE *UPANISHADS*

These date from around the sixth century BC (these texts could be regarded as late Vedas). There are over 100 *Upanishad* texts: some are very short (eighteen verses), while the oldest are over 100 pages long. The word "Upanishad" implies sitting at the feet of a master. Many of these texts contain conversations between a teacher and his disciples on mystical topics. Where the Vedas are mainly about ritual action – what you do – the *Upanishads* are more inward looking or theoretical, and they introduce some of the main concepts of Hinduism. For example, these texts develop monistic ideas, that is, "everything is one". The idea of *atman* (true self, first principle) and *Brahman* (absolute ground of existence) are sourced from the *Upanishads*.

Ramayana dancers, Java, Indonesia.

Smriti Texts

These consist of the memorized texts that sages have passed on to their followers.

THE *DHARMA SHASTRAS*

Dating from between the sixth and third centuries BC, these are the texts that outline social ritual and Hindu relationships. They uphold the Hindu caste hierarchy and contain the laws and duties regarding purity regulations (and hence social obligations). These regulations are the way to *moksha* – liberation from the continual cycle of life and death (*samsara*).

THE *RAMAYANA* AND THE *MAHABHARATA*

These epic poems are influenced by wars dating from the third to the first centuries BC. Because they have a plot, they are easily turned into dance, drama, and recitation. The *Mahabharata* contains the popular devotional text called the *Bhagavad Gita* – a conversation between the god Krishna and the warrior Arjuna in Arjuna's chariot on the eve of war with Arjuna's cousins. They talk of *karma* (cause and effect) and *dharma* (duty).

A scene from the *Bhagavad Gita* on a Hindu temple wall depicts Arjuna and the god Krishna at the battle of Kurukshetra.

The Call to Dharma

When Arjuna is on the battlefield, facing his cousins in battle, Lord Krishna counsels Arjuna to do his caste duty (*dharma*) as warrior (*Kshatriya*), above devotion to family.

This Life within all living things, my Prince!
Hides beyond harm; scorn thou to suffer, then,
For that which cannot suffer. Do thy part!
Be mindful of thy name, and tremble not!
Nought better can betide a martial soul
Than lawful war; happy the warrior
To whom comes joy of battle – comes, as now,
Glorious and fair, unsought; opening for him
A gateway unto Heav'n. But, if thou shunn'st
This honourable field – a Kshattriya –
If, knowing thy duty and thy task, thou bidd'st
Duty and task go by – that shall be sin!

Bhagavad Gita, *Book 2, Book of Doctrines*

THE *PURANAS*

Developed between the first and tenth centuries AD, these texts describe the appearances of the gods (*avatars*), and deal with the conquering of evil and the revival of good.

THE COSMIC MYTH

A key idea in Hinduism is the unity of all things. A creation text from the Vedas illustrates how the cosmos, society, and the human body are all related.

When they divided Purusa [the Cosmic Man], how many ways did they apportion him? What was his mouth? What were his arms? What were his thighs, his feet declared to be?

His mouth was the Brahmin [caste], his arms were the Rajanaya [Kshatriya, warrior caste], his thighs the Vaisya [artisan caste]; from his feet the Sudra [servant caste] was born.

The moon was born from his mind; from his eye the sun was born; from his mouth both Indra and Agni [fire]; from his breath Vayu [wind] was born.

From his navel arose the air; from his head the heavens evolved; from his feet the earth; the [four] directions from his ear. Thus, they fashioned the worlds.

"Purusa" (Hymn of Man): Rig Veda (Book 10, Hymn 90)

THE *TANTRAS*

Developed between the sixth and seventh centuries AD, these are manuals of techniques that claim to give direct and immediate spiritual experience of a shared universal consciousness. Some Hindus condemn these texts, as they perceive them to undermine the traditions of the Vedas. Some streams of Buddhism also call on the *Tantras*.

Hinduism

THE KEY IDEAS

Even though Hinduism has a very long history and many sacred texts, some of the key ideas are common to all strands.

DHARMA

Dharma has a very broad range of meanings. It can mean teaching, law, truth, providence, ethics, and religion. At a higher level, it means the moral force that holds the universe together. It is also the force that holds society together. At the individual level, it is the social obligation to behave according to one's *varna*, the social class into which one was born; therefore it can mean social duty.

CASTE AND CLASS

Derived from the ancient Vedas, Hinduism divides all peoples into four classes, or *varna*. In descending order, these are:

- the *Brahmin* (the priests and teachers, who lead Vedic sacrifices and rituals and do the teaching)
- the *Kshatriya* (the warriors and protectors of the people)
- the *Vaishya* (the commoners: merchants, agricultural workers)
- the *Sudra* (the lowly workers and serfs)

Those who are outside the four *varna* are called literally "out-castes" or "untouchables". Mahatma Gandhi wished to honour these people with the name *Harijan* ("children of God"). They call themselves *Dalit* (meaning "crushed and broken").

KARMA AND MOKSHA

Meaning "cause and effect", *karma* operates at an individual level. A person's present status in life – the social position into which they were born, as well as what they experience today – is determined by the law of *karma*. That is, today's experiences are determined by deeds done previously, even in a previous life. Simplistically, the law of *karma* could be reduced to "do good, get good; do bad, get bad". It follows then that today's behaviours will determine future outcomes; therefore, *karma* also means actions or works. The consequences of actions in this life extend to the nature of one's rebirth in the next life.

Karma implies bondage to this life, and *moksha* is the liberation from that bondage. Through practising austerities, meditation, renunciation, and other disciplines, one can overcome the entanglements of this world and find a deep sense of peace. *Moksha* is the final liberation of one's *atman* (loosely understood to mean "soul") from *samsara* (the cycle of birth and death), into union with the ultimate *Brahman* (ground of existence or being), like a drop of water falling into the ocean.

RITUAL

According to *dharma* there is a tension between the duties of worldly life on the one hand, and the renunciation of the world on the other. Because of this, there is a distinction drawn between the householder and the renouncer (*sanyasin*). The role of the householder is to uphold the social order through special rituals. The world renouncer is someone who leaves the social world of ritual obligations to seek liberation (*moksha*) from the endless cycle of reincarnation through life and death (*samsara*).

ATMAN

Usually translated as "soul", *atman* has two meanings: it is "Soul" in the sense of ultimate One-ness and also "soul" in the sense of an individual soul. Individual souls are all part of ultimate *atman*, or Soul. This is sometimes referred to as *Brahman*, that is, *Brahman* is the source of *atman*. Hence, because there is no difference between *Brahman* and *atman*, one finds ultimate reality (some would say "God"), by looking within oneself. Hinduism at its core is monistic: everything is one. For Hindus the idea of differentiation (that is, you and I are different) is an illusion.

BELIEF IN A TRANSCENDENT GOD

While the idea of *atman* is a monistic framework for Hinduism, there is nonetheless the idea of God in the term *Brahman*, ultimate reality. The sacred is experienced as both the impersonal *Brahman*, as well as in a devotional relationship with gods who have personality and can act in an

individual's life. These gods are understood to be lesser expressions of *Brahman*. Hence devotion (*bhakti*) to the gods is widespread in Hinduism. Krishna, an *avatar* of Vishnu is a popular god, and is easily recognized by his blue skin.

REINCARNATION

Reincarnation, the transmigration of the soul, is an important part of Hindu belief. Because everything is one, each person's individual *atman* can transmigrate through or within ultimate *atman*, that is, *Brahman*. When one dies, one is reincarnated according to the law of *karma*: in theory, either to a better existence or a worse one, depending on the balance of good and bad deeds. If one has

not intentionally sought during one's life to gain some karmic credit through good deeds, then the law of *karma* will be punitive.

HOLINESS AND THE SACRED

Central to Hinduism is the idea of the sacred and the profane. The everyday world is profane, that is, impure and polluted. The sacred is "pure" and brings good luck. Various rituals, people, and places (the Ganges river, for example) act as mediators between the two: statues/idols, temples, priests, even some special cities (Varanasi and Hardwar, for example) are channels of the sacred. Because of this, pilgrimage is important in Hinduism: one might travel to the holy city of Varanasi, so as to bathe in the Ganges River to wash away sin.

Puja is acts of worship. Hindus will perform *puja* regularly, or at auspicious times and places. It may be as simple an act as lighting a butter lamp or pouring water into a river; it may be more formal like visiting a temple and reciting texts, or saying prayers and requesting blessings from priests. These women, above, are performing *puja* in the River Ganges in India.

Hinduism

SOCIETY AND VILLAGE LIFE

The idea of *dharma* (religious and social duty) determines the way Hinduism orders its social structure. *Varna*, the four classes of society taught in the Vedic scriptures, shapes life in the village in strict ways. There is a vertical hierarchy of the four *varna*, but the lower three classes are also divided into castes, or *jati*.

Jati

Jati determine the role or job one has: *jati* sometimes look like trade guilds. However, governed by ritual purity laws, members of the same *jati* traditionally live and work together. For example, within the *Sudra* class (*varna*) – that is, the serfs and tradesmen – there are numerous *jati*, such as carpenters, blacksmiths, barbers, potters, and agricultural workers. So-called "out-castes" (that is, "those outside caste") or "untouchables", might include basket makers, tanners, sweepers, grave diggers, and toilet cleaners. There is only very rare intermarriage between *jati*, although this is becoming more common in cities today.

Caste Obligation

Dharma is one's duty to their caste: this is called *varna-dharma*. Not only is it a personal duty ("I am and always will be a *Rajput*/soldier"), but also a duty to where the caste "fits" hierarchically. If born a *Rajput* (a caste within the *Kshatriya* class), then it is one's duty (*dharma*) to be a good soldier. One must marry within the caste. However, because of being a soldier, one also has a duty (*dharma*) to protect the rest of society, particularly of those above – the Brahmin priests.

Purity and Segregation

Because ritual purity is so important, the management of physical space is crucial. A village will have set areas where different castes live: the *Brahmins* will be at the eastern end (towards the rising sun), then the *Kshatriya*, *Vaishya*, and *Sudra* spaced progressively westward. In the far west, often completely outside the village, will live the "out-castes" – those who do the ritually impure jobs serving the higher castes. There may even be different wells for each class.

APPROXIMATE CASTES SHARE OF POPULATION OF INDIA

- Brahmin (highest priestly caste) 5%
- Others (Buddhists or Christians) 9%
- Muslims 10%
- Scheduled tribes 13%
- Other upper castes 21%
- Other backward Castes 28%

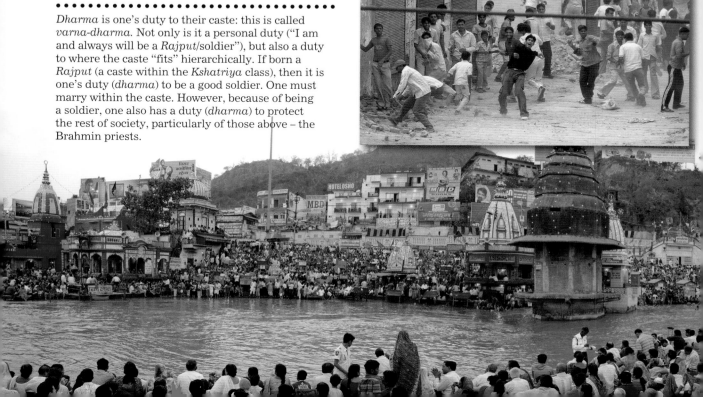

An Ideal Existence

Hindu society is ordered not only vertically, but it is also structured horizontally (or rather, chronologically). We could therefore think of *dharma* as ritual and moral behaviour coming together. The idea is for one to progress through a series of spiritual phases so as to live a good life. This is called *ashrama-dharma*, or duty to expressing an ideal caste lifespan. It roughly follows this order:

1. Celibate student (*brahmacharya*): This is the time of life associated with being single and focusing on education, especially learning one's duty to religion.

2. Householder (*grhastha*): The period when one focuses on earning a living and raising a family, as an expression of religious duty.

3. Forest dweller (*vanaprasha*): This is the time of "retirement", when one withdraws from the burdens of family life and shares the wisdom learned in life with others.

4. Renouncer (*sanyasa*): This phase is marked by a single-minded withdrawal from the world and the intentional seeking of *moksha* (liberation), through meditation.

Ideally, each of the four stages is twenty-five years long. Obviously not everyone is able to do this due to circumstances and resources. But it does stand as an ideal.

Left: Protesters from India's ethnic Gujjar community throwing stones at police and security personnel in 2007. They had blocked the highway in the outskirts of Delhi and demanded classification as a scheduled tribe, which would allow them to receive quotas set aside for disadvantaged sections of society and lower castes under India's affirmative action policy.

Rural v. Urban Life

Purity and caste rules dictate daily rituals in a village. These include *bhakti* (acts of devotion to the gods at home or at a village shrine) and rituals to improve good fortune. Astrology is important for determining auspicious times. Visits to temples (perhaps a village god or goddess), and participation in the various Hindu festivals mark the rhythm of the year. For difficulties and crises, a villager may look beyond the *Brahmin* priests to informal exorcists or diviners.

In urban India, caste rules are being challenged. There is more intermarriage between castes, as well as some upward mobility. Thus families may find themselves caught in the tension of living in a globalized world, but with the tug of traditional Hindu values.

Hinduism and Politics

The relationship between Hinduism and politics is growing. For example, the Indian government has assigned public sector jobs to the "scheduled castes" – that is, the lower castes (the *Dalit*), and legislated tighter parameters for their rights (for example, the Recognition of Forest Rights Act, 2006). In addition, Hindu political movements, such as the *Bharatiya Janata* Party (BJP), have growing influence due to their explicit and fundamentalist interpretations of Hinduism, particularly in response to the perceived threat of globalization and modernism.

HINDU FESTIVALS

There are many different festivals in India. Most are in honour of various gods, both "main" gods and local deities. People celebrate the deities' birthdays, marriages, or various important events. There are also many regional festivals. Many are tied to the seasons, and can be set by either lunar or solar calendars. Some are also celebrated by Jains and Sikhs.

■ **Holi**: This is a festival of the god Vishnu that occurs in the spring (March). There are bonfires, and people throw coloured and scented powders and water at each other.

■ **Diwali**: This is the "festival of lights" occurring sometime between mid-October and mid-December. It honours Lakshmi, goddess of wealth, and is celebrated as a family event. It also celebrates victory of good over evil, represented by house cleaning, wearing new clothes, lighting lamps, setting off fireworks, and consuming lots of sweets.

■ **Khumbh mela**: The timing and location of this festival is determined by the stars. It is celebrated every twelve years, with smaller ones every six years. Pilgrims attend in their millions. It is a purification festival: bathing in the holy river at an auspicious time washes away sins. Allahabad and Nasik are two locations where the Khumbh mela is usually held.

Left: Pilgrims attend the Aarti ceremony in which light from wicks soaked in ghee (purified butter) or camphor is offered to one or more deities, during the Kumbh mela in Haridwar.

Hinduism

INFLUENCE IN THE WEST

Hinduism is a collection of ideas, philosophies, rituals, and gods without one overall belief, founder, or story. "Hinduism" as a religion is something that the British invented when they tried to name and identify this rainbow of beliefs and practices when ruling India between the eighteenth and twentieth centuries.

Buddhism, Jainism, and Sikhism all have commonality with Hinduism. In addition, the indigenous tribes of India that have their own "primal" religions often overlap considerably with Hinduism, because "things Hindu" are the very air of the Indian subcontinent.

Hinduism also found a welcome home in Western countries in the 1960s. George Harrison's "My Sweet Lord" is essentially a song of devotion to the Hindu god Krishna. Yoga, popular in the West mainly for meditation and exercise, comes from Hinduism. The sexual revolution of the 1960s was informed partly by readings from the Hindu book *Kama Sutra*. Hindu *Sankya* philosophy has informed Western philosophy, leading many to adopt ideas of reincarnation and *karma*.

Hindu Sects in the West

The International Society of Krishna Consciousness (ISKCON), more commonly known as the "Hare Krishnas", is an easily recognizable Hindu sect. On many streets in Western cities, members chant devotional songs to Krishna, hand out tracts, and engage people in conversation. Founded in 1965 by A. C. Bhaktivedanta Swami Prabhupada, the "Hare Krishnas" have enough momentum in the West to build and sustain temples and residential teaching centres. Charismatic *gurus* (teachers) also came to the West in the 1960s and 1970s, founding other high-profile movements such as Transcendental Meditation, The Self-Realization Fellowship, and Satya Sai Baba Society.

In addition, because of extensive migration and globalization, it is not uncommon now to find Hindu temples in Western cities: these temples often become the focus for Indian communities, and represent the particular heritage and religious tradition of those communities. In any Western city today, there may be different temples devoted to different deities. Thus the Hindu deities – Krishna, Shiva, Vishnu, Parvati, Sarasvati, Laxmi, Rama, Hanuman, and Ganesh – are now much more visible in the West. The prevalence of shrines, as well as pictures and statuettes of the gods – often visible in Indian shops – shows that these deities and their devotees are no longer confined to their cultural and religious contexts of the Indian subcontinent.

YOGA

Yoga is a technique associated with Hindu *Sankya* philosophy to "control, yoke, unite" rigorous body discipline and meditation so as to gain insight into the nature of reality. While based on a number of Hindu texts, yoga has come to be a form of body postures – now marketed in the West as physical exercise – whereby the mind and senses are disciplined and controlled in a way that allows the limitations of one's ego to be overcome. This transformation seeks to remove mental impurities, such as greed and hate. Yoga assumes seven *chakras*, or power points, descending down the line of symmetry of the body through which spiritual energy is channelled. Apart from the physical exercise, it is attractive to many in the West due to its claim to help people to realize their true identity.

● SEE ALSO
BUDDHISM PP. 46–53
JAINISM PP. 98–99
SIKHISM PP. 102–103

Children at Janmashtami festival (Krishna's birthday) at Bhaktivedanta Manor ISKCON (Hare Krishna) temple, Watford, UK.

TANTRA

Tantra refers to a collection of Indian texts that appeared around the sixth century AD in India. These texts outline techniques for gaining powers through yoga practice: for example, the power to fly, walk through walls, and turn metals into gold. More realistically, *tantra* offers personal empowerment.

The word *tantra* derives from "loom" or "weaving", with the idea of creating something by meshing together two items (the warp and the woof). In a broader sense it suggests expansion and continuity.

In tantric exercises, the person experiences an expansion of consciousness by unifying opposites: this is achieved through a variety of means, including the use of ritual symbols, gestures, patterns, and words. Additionally, when negative (represented as female) and positive (represented as male) energies are united, this liberates the mind and body from the endless cycle of existence (*samsara*). In other words, this is a path to *moksha* (liberation). Hence sexual expression in *tantra* is not uncommon: the Hindu gods Shiva and Shakti (Parvati) are depicted in sitting copulation; the *yoni-lingam* (the phallus within the womb) is venerated.

Tantrism has a countercultural impulse in it. Because of the strong feminine theme, *tantra* in the West has combined with Wicca, witchcraft, paganism, angelology, yoga, goddess movements, and also alchemy. Common to these movements is the raising of sexual energy. Hence Western expressions of *tantra* are sometimes known as "sacred sex", and overlap with various sexual psychologies.

HINDUISM AND HOLLYWOOD

The *Star Wars* films (1977–2005) and *Avatar* (2009) have the Hindu idea of *Brahman* in them – that is, that the ultimate reality is one. "Avatar" itself is a Hindu term meaning the gods becoming human, and the use of the colour blue in the film is consistent with the colour of Hindu avatars (Krishna being the most obvious). Other films also draw on Hindu ideas. *Groundhog Day* (1993) plays on the theme of *karma*, in that one might be able to control one's next "incarnation". *The Matrix* (1999) contains a pot pourri of Eastern themes. Its exploration of the nature of reality hints at Hindu philosophical ideas.

Buddhism

THE LIFE OF THE BUDDHA

There are somewhere between 360 and 800 million Buddhists in the world. Originating in northern India in the fifth century BC, Buddhism spread throughout northern and eastern Asia. In the mid-twentieth century Buddhism suddenly became a global phenomenon, influenced in part by the exile of the Dalai Lama from Tibet in 1959. Consequently, it is sometimes helpful to think of Buddhism in two ways: the Buddhism of those brought up in the religion in Asia, and that of those who converted to it outside Asia, particularly in the West.

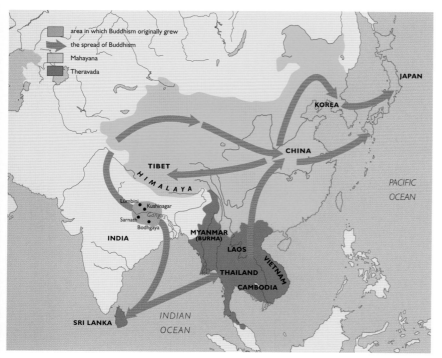

Map shows the spread of Buddhism and geographical differentiation into its two current forms: Theravada and Mahayana.

Is Buddhism a Religion?

While having "family resemblances" with other religions, some people argue that Buddhism is not actually a religion at all. They might see it as a psychology, a philosophy, or a meditation tool. In Western contexts, this can lead to people combining their own interpretations of Buddhism with other religions.

Common Threads

A core teaching is common to all Buddhist schools. All agree that the Buddha was an Indian prince of the fifth century BC. He became enlightened and taught the Four Noble Truths. From this central idea many different beliefs and rituals radiate out across Asia. For example, some of the spiritual "air" of India influences Buddhism, including *karma*, renunciation, meditation, and reincarnation; however, Buddhists interpret these differently to Hindus.

Buddha's Beginnings

The Buddha was born Siddhartha Gautama, or Sakyamuni, prince of the Sakya clan, in northern India sometime between the sixth and fifth centuries BC. Sources vary significantly on the details of his life, but the following gives a general idea of what Buddhists believe are the significant events.

Queen Mahamaya dreamed one night of a silver elephant entering her womb from the side. Hindu Brahmin priests foretold a son who would become either a king or a Buddha – an enlightened one. In the village of Lumbini, Queen Mahamaya gave birth to a son, Siddhartha, on the full moon of May. Siddhartha was raised a prince, and was protected from the world. At sixteen Siddhartha married his cousin Yasodhara. However, at twenty-nine, Siddhartha was exposed to the "Four Sights". He first saw an old man, then a sick man, and then a corpse. His charioteer explained that all people are subject to old age, sickness, and death. The fourth sight was an ascetic man – someone who has renounced the world – and Siddhartha was impressed by his peaceful nature. Siddhartha decided to renounce his princely home and adopt the ascetic's austere lifestyle in hope of finding peace among all the suffering he had observed.

● SEE ALSO

HINDUISM PP. 42–43   JAINISM PP. 98–99
BUDDHISM PP. 50–51   SIKHISM PP. 102–103
CHINESE RELIGION PP. 54–55

BUDDHA'S "GREAT RENUNCIATION"

After Siddhartha left his sleeping wife and son one night ("The Great Renunciation"), he crossed over the river, adopted the ascetics' ways, and wandered around northern India. Learning from Hindu sages, and seeking truth, he attracted a small band of disciples. However, he remained unsatisfied, subjecting himself to severe austerities to the point of nearly starving himself to death. Still, he remained unconvinced that this was the path to truth.

THE ENLIGHTENMENT

Siddhartha resolved then to sit beneath a tree until he experienced enlightenment. This happened while he was in a state of deep meditation: he became the Buddha, the enlightened one, finally realizing the path to the end of suffering.

The Buddha then reassembled his original five disciples near the Indian city of Varanasi. They were sceptical: how could he have attained enlightenment without all the physical trials of the ascetics' disciplines? Nevertheless, the Buddha preached his first sermon, which outlined the way to end suffering. He argued that the Eightfold Path was a "middle way" between the extremes of Hindu asceticism and princely indulgence. This first sermon, called "Setting in Motion of the Wheel of Truth", occurred at the deer park in Sarnath. Subsequently, the Buddha spent the rest of his life wandering northern India with a growing band of disciples, teaching the *dharma* – the truth he had discovered.

At Kushinagar, the Buddha lay on his right side and experienced *parinirvana* (death) at age eighty (c. 400 BC).

THE EXAMPLE OF THE BUDDHA

The sequence of events in the life of the Buddha is regarded as an ideal pattern to follow by some Buddhists. They might renounce the world for a time of meditation and service. Alternatively, one family member (usually the oldest boy) is given for a time to the *sangha* – the community of monks and nuns. The ceremony of initiation into Buddhism is called "taking refuge in the Three Jewels" (that is, the Buddha, *dharma*, and *sangha*), and pilgrimage to the holy sites of the Buddha's life is thought to award pilgrims with karmic merit: Lumbini (Buddha's birthplace), Bodhgaya (place he reached enlightenment), Sarnath (where he gave his first sermon) and Kushinagar (place Buddha died). Wesak (*Vesakha*) is the main Buddhist festival, celebrating birth, enlightenment, and *parinirvana* (the Buddha's death) at the full moon in May.

The "Four Sights" of Siddharta depicted on painted silk: the old man, sick man, corpse, and ascetic.

Buddhism

A GLOBAL RELIGION

Following the Buddha's first sermon, the group of disciples grew from the original five to include a variety of relatives, princes, and lay people, including Gautama's (that is, the Buddha's) wife, Yasodhara. The Buddha rejected the hierarchy of the Hindu caste system and promoted a democratic ideal among his disciples. The rules for the *sangha* – this growing band of disciples – were collected and became the *vinaya*, meaning "the discipline". This later became an authoritative part of the original Buddhist scriptures, the Tripitaka.

Buddhism spread from India westward through the Khyber Pass into modern-day Afghanistan. The large Bamiyan Buddhas, destroyed by the Taliban in 2001, show there was a significant Buddhist presence in central Afghanistan from around AD 500. Buddhism also spread into Tibet, China, Korea, and Japan in the north, and down to Sri Lanka in the south, across to Thailand and the South East Asian peninsula. More recently, from the nineteenth century, Western scholars began translating Buddhist texts into European languages. In the latter half of the twentieth century, many different sects of Buddhism have found a home in many different countries around the globe.

The Role of the Buddhist Councils

About three months after the Buddha's death (c. 400 BC), a council was called to agree on the contents of the Buddha's teaching. This became known as the First Council. A Second Council followed about seventy years later, mainly to deal with the monks' indiscipline. Until this point the *sangha* – the community of monks – had the study of Buddha's teachings as their focus, but now practice (how does one live out this teaching?) was becoming important. Conflict at each of these councils resulted in disagreements. A clear split occurred in 250 BC at a Third Council. The issues were mainly around what writings were authoritative, and what should be compulsory rules for monks. While the issues were complex, it is clear that different groups of interpretation emerged.

Left: One of the Bamiyan Buddhas, before its destruction in 2001.

How Did Buddhism Spread?

Buddhism has spread around the world by four main means:

1. When the emperor or local officials endorsed, sponsored, and spread it: for example, Ashok (c. 304–232 BC), emperor of the Maurya dynasty in India; Songtsen Gampo (c. AD 618–50), of the Tibetan Yarlung dynasty; Kublai Khan (r. AD 1260–94), first Yuan emperor of China.

2. When migrants take their Buddhism with them. Recent examples include the movement of Tibetan lamas (priests or monks) out from Tibet into the West from 1959, and the emigration of Hong Kong residents before 1997.

3. When believers and practitioners return to a Buddhist nation and recruit and "fetch" Buddhism. Japanese scholars went to China to translate and acquire Buddhist texts – both Chan (to become Zen) and Pure Land texts – from as early as AD 252. When new Buddhist groups are established in the West today, they often recruit a Buddhist teacher from Asia.

4. When sects have missionary zeal. Sokkai Gakai is an example of an intentionally missionary sect of Buddhism: as a renewal movement informed by Japanese culture it actively promotes itself and recruits new members. Friends of the Western Buddhist Order (renamed Triratna in 2010) and New Kadampa Tradition are two sects that intentionally create an attractive presence in Western countries so as to recruit new members.

Taking Refuge

For a religion to spread, people must be able to become an adherent or worshipper within that religion. They must be able to "convert" to it somehow. How then does one "become" a Buddhist?

A person "takes refuge" as an initiation rite into Buddhism. This is usually a short and simple ceremony in which the initiate says in front of a monk or teacher the threefold confession:

I take refuge in the Buddha.
I take refuge in the dharma.
I take refuge in the sangha.

These three respectively refer to the person and/or ideal of the Buddha as enlightened, the truth of how things really are (the *dharma*), and the community of practising monks and nuns, or even the wider Buddhist community (*sangha*).

In some Buddhist sects, this threefold confession is said as part of the ordination rites when a person becomes a monk or nun. Some in the West would consider themselves Buddhist, even if they haven't formally "taken refuge".

Western Buddhists pray for peace and compassion.

On the third and final day of the Poi Sang Long festival, when novice monks are initiated, young boys give up their princes' costumes, exchanging them for monks' robes.

Buddhism

THE FOUR TRUTHS AND BUDDHIST TEXTS

All Buddhist sects recognize (to various degrees) the central teaching of the Four Noble Truths. When the prince Siddhartha Gautama (also known as Sakyamuni) was enlightened, it is these four truths that came together in his mind, resulting in the "aha!" moment he had beneath the tree in Bodhgaya (north India). In other words, he was "awakened" to this particular way of understanding how and why there was suffering in the world, and also to a way of dealing with the suffering.

The Four Noble Truths

1. The first truth: existence is *dukka* (suffering).
2. The second truth: *dukka* is caused by *tanha* (desire or craving).
3. The third truth: liberation from suffering and craving is possible by eliminating desire (*nirvana*).
4. The fourth truth: the way to get release from desire is by following the Eightfold Path. The Eightfold path is:

- right view
- right thought
- right speech
- right action
- right living
- right endeavour
- right mindfulness
- right concentration

The four truths are at the heart of the *dharma. Dharma* can mean "religion", "teaching", or "truth". A *dharma* teacher would teach the Four Noble Truths, or he might also teach from any of the numerous Buddhist texts.

Buddhist Sources/Literature

The scriptures of Buddhism are in various languages. Many texts are in Pali, an ancient Indian language that is not spoken today: it is thought that these texts may be closer to what the Buddha actually said. These texts have been translated, and others added, such that a body of Buddhist literature exists in Pali, Sanskrit, Tibetan, Chinese, and Japanese. In addition there is now a growing number of texts originating in European languages: these are either new, or commentaries on the classical Asian texts, or translations of them.

Unlike Christianity, Judaism, or Islam, Buddhism does not have one authoritative book. Rather, there is a broad selection of *sutras* (*sutta* in Pali) – that is, religious texts. The word *sutra* carries the idea of "thread", in the sense of continuity and tradition over a long period of time. Various schools and sects of Buddhism give priority to different *sutras*. Indeed, some sects are defined precisely because they prioritize one particular *sutra*.

However, Buddhist sects and individuals might have favourite *sutras* that are condensed and transportable. The Dhamapadda is a favourite collection of proverbs, for example. Other widely read *sutras* and texts are the Metta Sutra, the Heart Sutra, the Diamond Sutra, the Songs of Milarepa, and the Lam Rim. In addition, Buddhism has a collection of folk tales – the Jataka tales – which are similar to Aesop's fables. They are short stories based on common events in life that are designed to teach moral truths or promote right behaviours.

The Great Buddha statue, Bodhgaya, Bihar, India.

● SEE ALSO
BUDDHISM PP. 44–45
BUDDHISM PP. 50–51

THE PALI CANON

The Pali Canon ("canon" means an authoritative body of scriptures by which other scriptures are measured) is a sacred text for Theravada Buddhists. Many Mahayana Buddhists also hold it as sacred. It has three sections or "baskets" (*pitaka*).

■ First basket: Vinaya Pitaka (rules for conduct of the *sangha*, the Buddhist community).

■ Second basket: Sutta Pitaka (thousands of discourses, that is, teachings of the Buddha).

■ Third basket: Abhidhamma Pitaka (a commentary and reworking of the *sutras*).

MAHAYANA SCRIPTURES

Mahayana sects recognize the Pali Canon (or a translation of it), but also have hundreds of additional sutras, some of which are common to all Mahayana sects, and some of which are unique to each sect. For example, Pure Land Buddhism gives special priority to the Sukhavativyuha Sutras.

A 1st-century plaque decorated with a scene from the Jataka tales with Ekacringa and Princess Nalini, from Begram, Afghanistan.

TIBETAN BUDDHISM

Tibetan Buddhism has two large collections of texts called the Kanjur and the Tanjur. This can be such a number of volumes that when bound and placed on a bookshelf, it would cover the whole wall of an average-sized room. It is a collection of texts from Pali and Mahayana sources, as well as new and innovative Tibetan texts.

THE HEART SUTRA

The Heart Sutra is one of the more important *sutras* in Mahayana Buddhism as it presents the core idea of emptiness.

Thus have I heard… Form is emptiness; emptiness also is form. Emptiness is no other than form; form is no other than emptiness. In the same way, feeling, perception, formation and consciousness are emptiness. Thus, Shariputra, all dharmas are emptiness. There are no characteristics. There is no birth and no cessation. There is no impurity and no purity. There is no decrease and no increase. Therefore, Shariputra, in emptiness, there is no form, no feeling, no perception, no formation, no consciousness …

Buddhism

SECTS AND MOVEMENTS

Buddhism has three main groups: Theravada, Mahayana, and Vajrayana (Tibetan). While they have a common core – for example, upholding the Four Noble Truths – these groups differ in their teachings and rituals, their location, and their history.

Theravada Buddhism

Theravada Buddhism is the oldest group, with teachings that are closest to the original teachings of the Buddha, dating approximately from the Third Buddhist Council of 250 BC. Theravada Buddhism tends to be conservative: it emphasizes attaining liberation by one's own efforts, with a strong emphasis on following the core scriptures of Buddhism – the *dhamma* (*dharma*) – as a guide. Theravada Buddhists are generally in the southern and south-eastern countries of Asia, namely Sri Lanka, Myanmar (Burma), Thailand, Cambodia, Laos, and Vietnam. Theravada Buddhism informs Vipassana meditation and Insight Meditation found in the West.

THE *STUPA*

The mound-shaped *stupa* (or *chorten*) is a common Buddhist structure. Broadly similar across all Buddhist sects, it is a type of reliquary for various precious objects. Originally, it would have contained the remains of the Buddha himself, but today it might house the bones of a famous teacher. Before a *stupa* is commissioned it is usually packed with, and hence "empowered" by, significant objects like copies of scriptures. A *stupa* might also commemorate an event or person. The shape of it symbolizes the *dharma*, that is, Buddhist teaching. Overall, a *stupa* is generally constructed as a place and object of devotion at which a Buddhist may gain merit or experience spiritual power. Below is the stupa of the Swayambhunath temple, Kathmandu, Nepal.

● SEE ALSO
BUDDHISM PP. 44–45

Mahayana Buddhism

This movement began somewhere around the first century AD. Maha-yana means "great vehicle" or "great way". It introduced many new teachings to Buddhism, and tends to still be creative in its teaching. For example, it accepts a much broader number of scriptures than Theravada Buddhism. Mahayana has saviour figures and has developed some sophisticated and complex philosophies. It is less concerned with historical particulars, such as the dates and actual teachings of the historical Buddha. Because of this innovative tendency, Mahayanists refer to the conservative Buddhists (the Theravadans) as Hinayanists (those of the "lesser vehicle"). Mahayana Buddhism can be found in countries of east Asia, specifically China, Korea, and Japan.

Vajrayana Buddhism

This is the "diamond vehicle", and some would place this expression of Buddhism within Mahayana. It developed from the sixth century AD in India, but has become associated mainly with Tibet, Nepal, Bhutan, Mongolia, and a few smaller movements (for example, Shingon Buddhism in Japan). Sometimes it is simply known as "Tibetan Buddhism" or "northern Buddhism". It is based in part on Mahayana teachings, but also draws on Tantra, the original Tibetan Bön religion, and Siberian shamanism. Vajrayana has developed religious disciplines based on meditation and teacher lineage, and has also developed the idea of saviour figures – *bodhisattvas* – to a high degree. From the early 1960s, new expressions of Tibetan Buddhist schools have become widely spread throughout the West.

The *Arhat* and the *Bodhisattva* Ideals

In Theravada Buddhism, the *arhat* is a person who has attained *nibbana* (*nirvana*), where attachment, hatred, and delusion are forever destroyed. Not all *arhats* are the same: some are teachers, some are extraordinary meditators (with psychic powers), and some live an ascetic lifestyle. The "*arhat* ideal" is sometimes criticized as being very individualistic.

In Mahayana Buddhism, the *bodhisattva* is a being who is worthy of *nirvana* but puts it off, and, in acts of compassion, transfers their karmic credit to others. A *bodhisattva* may be a human being or a heavenly saviour figure. Hence the "*bodhisattva* ideal" – unique to Mahayana Buddhism and highly developed in Tibetan/Vajrayana Buddhism – offers an assisted path to *nirvana*, as well as an opportunity for people to develop ethics of compassion. In wisdom and by "skilful means" the *bodhisattva* can work for the salvation of all sentient beings, that is, those beings with consciousness.

The Dalai Lama is technically the leader only of the Gelugpa sect of Tibetan Buddhism, but in practice he is spiritual head of the whole of Tibetan Buddhism. He is a living *bodhisattva*, a reincarnation of the deity Avalokateshvara. The Dalai Lama gave up his leadership of the Tibetan government in exile to an elected prime minister in 2011. Being a Nobel Peace Prize winner (1989), he continues travelling widely and promoting peace and compassion.

EXAMPLES OF BUDDHIST SECTS

THERAVADAN BUDDHIST SCHOOLS

1. Vipassana meditation
2. The Thai Forest tradition
3. Insight Meditation

MAHAYANA BUDDHIST SCHOOLS

4. Zen (Ch'an in China, and Son in Korea)
5. Pure Land
6. Soka Gakkai
7. New Kadampa Tradition
8. Foundation for the Preservation of the Mahayana Tradition (FPMT)
9. The Western Buddhist Order (now Triratna)

TIBETAN/VAJRAYANA BUDDHIST SCHOOLS

10. Shingon (Japan)
11. Tibetan Buddhism has four main sects: Nyingmapa, Sakyapa, Kagyupa, and Gelugpa

Buddhism

A WESTERN PHENOMENON

Buddhism started arriving in the West in the 1800s, when European colonial explorers and scholars translated many Buddhist texts. In 1893 Ceylonese Buddhist reformer Anagarika Dharmapala (1864–1933) attended the World Parliament of Religions in Chicago; he could be regarded as the founder of American Buddhism. Further contact with Buddhists from Asia was because of immigration (for example, the Japanese to America from the 1850s), and because some Chinese worked in the gold rushes (California, 1848; Victoria, Australia, 1851; Otago, New Zealand, from 1866).

However, there was a real explosion of interest in Buddhism in the West in the 1960s. This was due in

part to the Dalai Lama's flight from Tibet into India in 1959 following the Chinese takeover of his homeland. Tibetan lamas and refugees also fled Tibet and took up residence in Western countries, many founding teaching centres. In addition, Westerners found Zen Buddhism attractive in the 1950s and 1960s. These first expressions of interest in Buddhism were chiefly in America, but interest slowly grew in Western Europe and then in other Western nations.

Today, there are a vast number of Buddhist traditions and lineages that have grown rapidly in the West. For both the United States and Australia, census data from 2000 onwards shows that Buddhism is the fastest growing religion. Los Angeles now has every tradition of Buddhism represented in it.

New Western Expressions of Buddhism

Engaged Buddhism has gained momentum because of its strong social–ethical impulse: it is Buddhism "engaged" with the social issues in the West, such as poverty, war, and the environment. Green Buddhism, Feminist Buddhism, Black Buddhism, and Gay Buddhism are all now recognizable movements. We can also talk of American Buddhism, German Buddhism, or Australian Buddhism: these are unique cultural expressions.

BUDDHISM AND HOLLYWOOD

The life of Buddha was popularized in the West through Sir Edwin Arnold's epic poem *The Light of Asia* (1908) and Herman Hesse's book *Siddhartha* (English translation, 1951). Conrad Rook's 1972 film version of *Siddhartha* was re-released in 2002. The number of films about Buddhism has increased remarkably in the 1990s. These films are mainly ones with Tibetan themes: *Little Buddha* (1994), *Seven Years in Tibet* (1997), *Kundun* (1997), and *The Cup* (2000). Films with Buddhist elements have been produced too. For example the Star Wars saga has an underlying monism that can be argued to be Buddhist. (Its director, George Lucas, is a Buddhist.)

"Celebrity Buddhists" in both Hollywood and the music industry boost the profile of Buddhism. Richard Gere, Steven Seagal, Tina Turner, Herbie Hancock, Uma Thurman, Sharon Stone, Harrison Ford, Orlando Bloom, Kate Bosworth, Goldie Hawn and Adam Yauch have all at some time been identified with Buddhism.

The Western media and celebrities promote Buddhism as a psychology, or a means to world peace and compassion, or simply as a cool trend. Western expressions of Buddhism are easily commercialized.

Differences Between Western and Asian Buddhism

It is generally accepted that Asian and Western Buddhism look different. In Western countries, we can talk of "immigrant Buddhism" (that which Asian immigrants bring with them) and "convert Buddhism" (the Buddhism that Western "converts" create for themselves). Some of the differences between Asian and Western Buddhism are highlighted below.

SPEED OF ESTABLISHMENT
Where it took hundreds – perhaps a thousand – years for Buddhism to be established in Asia, Buddhism has taken root in less than a decade in some Western countries.

VARIETY
In contrast to Asia, where distinct cultural Buddhist traditions have dominated one particular country (for example, Zen in Japan), the whole range of Buddhist traditions rub shoulder to shoulder in Western cities. This offers more choice and overlap among the groups themselves.

LEADERSHIP
Leadership structures are changing: the ordained monk in Asia, trained by years of rigorous teaching and ritual, has been replaced by the scholar lay leader in the West.

POLITICS
No country in the West has declared itself to be a Buddhist country or as having a Buddhist majority, unlike some Buddhist nations of Asia (such as Thailand, Bhutan, and Sri Lanka).

AUTHORITY
The Buddhist communities (*sangha*) in the West tend to be more democratic and egalitarian than their Asian counterparts, with women finding a stronger voice in leading Buddhist centres, teaching, and writing. This may also be because the laity is often highly educated.

VARIABLE TEACHING
Core beliefs vary: *karma*, reincarnation, and related doctrines are embraced in the West, but they vary in their interpretation from their Asian roots. The very idea of a set of core beliefs is rejected by some in the West. Many Western Buddhists pick and choose from different traditions.

Valley of the Temples, Japanese Buddhist Byodo-in Temple located in the Mountains of Oahu in Hawaii, USA.

Chinese Religions

THE THREE TEACHINGS

China has three main religions – Daoism, Buddhism, and Confucianism – which are sometimes called "The Three Teachings". In China, it is acceptable to talk of "Chinese Religion", and by this we mean a unique blend of the three. These three religions are not exclusive of each other, and there has been much merging and mingling of their teachings and rituals. They could be regarded as three parts of one overarching worldview. Confucianism in particular could be regarded as more of a social philosophy than a religion.

Each of the three religions does, however, have its own unique expression in temples, writings, and rituals. Additionally, each has a history of its own, and each has sought to gain the favour of the emperor from time to time, wanting to become the state religion. We can talk of Daoism and Buddhism as being religions of the common people, while Confucianism has been the philosophy of the state.

TEMPLE OF HEAVEN IN BEIJING

The emperor was considered to be a son of heaven, and he administered earthly matters on behalf of heaven. The Temple of Heaven was an altar where the emperor prayed for good harvests. In 1998 it was declared to be a UNESCO world heritage site.

The Influence of Buddhism

Confucianism and Daoism evolved initially (approximately the fifth to the second centuries BC) without significant contact with any other religion; hence, they developed unique ideas and practices. Debates between Confucians and Daoists within China helped shape their views, often clarifying how they were different. When Buddhism arrived from India in the first century BC, both were influenced: the Daoists took up the monastic and meditative traditions, and the Confucians revised and adapted their philosophy in light of Buddhism.

During the Ming dynasty (1369–1644), Lin Choa-en (1517–98) tried to harmonize the three religions into one, bringing together the strong Buddhist and Daoist monastic and meditative traditions with the Confucian concern for fellow humanity.

Other Influences

China has also been influenced by various denominations of Christianity (such as Eastern Syrian, Catholic, and Protestant). Islam is the religion of some large minorities within China, and the political ideologies of Republicanism and Communism dominated Chinese history in the twentieth century.

Nevertheless, the ideals of fusion, unity, and harmony permeate all aspects of the Chinese worldview. The main features of Chinese religion continue to be ethical behaviour, social relationships (with the living and with the ancestors), and self-realization.

● SEE ALSO
BUDDHISM PP. 46–53
DAOISM PP. 56–59
CONFUCIANISM PP. 60–65

COMMON IDEAS IN CHINESE "THREE RELIGIONS"

Daoism, Buddhism, and Confucianism share some common underlying principles. The following list is adapted from Ninian Smart's book, *The World's Religions* (1989).

Ch'an	Ch'an – meditation (derived from the Sanskrit/Indian term *dhyana*). It became the name of a meditation school, and is known in Japan as *Zen*.
Ch'i	Ch'i – energy or life force.
Ching	Ching – a generic word used for "religious text". While used for the classic five Confucian texts, it also is used for the *sutras* of Buddhism and the texts of Daoism.
T'ai Chi	T'ai Chi – the Supreme Ultimate in the *I Ching* (one of the oldest classical texts) and in neo-Confucianism. It is the source of all things.
T'ai P'ing	T'ai P'ing – heavenly peace or the end-times kingdom which Daoist literature in particular looks forward to. It is the name given to the Chinese revolutionaries of 1850–64 (hence "The Taiping Rebellion") who wanted to establish a new social order in China.
Tao	Tao – the Way. The principle through which nature works.
T'ien	T'ien – heaven. Heaven is deified and personalized. One of the key roles the Chinese emperor had was devotion to *T'ien* in order to ensure harmony of the cosmos and the well-being of society.
Yang	Yang – The male principle of the world. The harmony of *yin* and *yang* forms the basis for the Chinese worldview.
Yin	Yin – The female principle of the world.

YIN AND YANG

Opposites in Chinese thinking are not exclusive, but complementary. Hence female/male, dark/light, knowledge/ignorance, young/old, visible/invisible, cold/hot, water/fire, earth/air are interconnected and dependent on each other: they are complementary aspects of *yin* and *yang*. They give rise to each other and can only exist in relationship to each other. *Yin* and *yang* relate to the material world and have no moral qualities. The concept of good and evil as complements was developed later in a Confucian context with respect to the *yin* and *yang*. This Granite yin and yang symbol is located on the floor of the Chinese Garden of Friendship, Darling Harbour, Sydney, Australia.

EARLY CHINESE RELIGION

Chinese history extends back to around 4000 BC, when a civilization grew around the vast river system of the Yellow River and its tributaries. Society was based on agriculture, and, like Egypt and the Indus Valley civilizations, the river was regarded as a god who provided nutrition for crops, but who could also punish, as when the river flooded. Hence, although considered "the mother river", the Yellow River was regarded as both a blessing and a curse. The ancient Chinese believed the Yellow River flowed from heaven: it was a continuation of the Milky Way, and there are many legends of people undertaking spiritual journeys along the river in search of its heavenly source. It was during the Zhou dynasty (1046–256 BC) that the idea of a personified heaven emerged; hence the "mandate of heaven" was claimed thereafter by all subsequent emperors. Confucius was then able to readily bring together notions of order in the cosmos (heaven), the world around (the river and harvests), and social structure (the family).

Daoism

TEACHERS AND HISTORICAL DEVELOPMENT

In Chinese thought the word *Dao* or *Tao* means "the Way". Daoism is not an orderly religion of texts, beliefs, and rituals. Rather, it is a cluster of ideas derived from ancient sources in China, including various hermits who had a strong love of nature. Some call Daoism a "nature mysticism". In social terms, Daoism can be understood as nature verses the city, or China's rural south revolting against its urban north. Daoism is "this worldly", but Daoism says that we are not ourselves by living in concrete cities; rather, by living among the mountains we can get closer to the *Dao*, the Ultimate Way. To be truly human is not to be confined by social expectations but to have the freedom to roam in and with "the Way".

The Sage Lao-tzu

Lao-tzu was a Chinese sage whose life is shrouded in mystery and hence whose birth and death dates are difficult to verify. He probably lived in the sixth century BC (predating Confucius). He is generally considered to be the founder of Daoism.

THE *TAO-TE CHING*

The *Tao-te Ching* ("The Classic of the Way and Virtue") is traditionally attributed to Lao-tzu, though there is no consensus on when it was written. Sometimes the *Tao-te Ching* text is merely called *Lao-tzu*, after the name of its alleged author. The first half deals with the *Dao* (the Way), and the second half with the *Te* (inner strength or virtue).

The *Tao-te Ching* consists of eighty-one brief chapters comprised of short, pithy sayings and statements, often in poetic form. The topics range from political advice for rulers to daily practical wisdom for common people. Some sayings are intentional contradictions. There is only minimal punctuation and the text reads as if it is meant to be ambiguous. This is consistent with the Daoist way of wandering, and not being constricted by convention: the ideal spiritual life is to flourish, and flourishing is not achieved by being confined to the rules of language or the rules of society. The origin of all things, including one's own self, is found in nature, intuition, spontaneity, and freedom. Ambiguity and wandering are virtues.

The *Tao-te Ching* is the second most translated book in the world (after the Bible).

Daoists focus on the simplicity of life, rooted in the love of nature, which is shown in landscape paintings. This hanging scroll (ink on silk) dates from AD 990–1040 and is by Fan Ku'an.

● SEE ALSO
BUDDHISM PP. 46—53
CHINESE RELIGION PP. 54—55
CONFUCIANISM PP. 60—65

The Sage Chuang-tzu

Chuang-tzu's life, like Lao-tzu's, is shadowed by legend, although he may have lived at around the same time as Mencius, the disciple of Confucius (that is, around 300 BC). The main text attributed to him is called by his name, although it may have had multiple authors.

THE *CHUANG-TZU*

Unlike the *Tao-te Ching*, the *Chuang-tzu* is cynical about politics. It calls for a renunciation of social conventions, but it does this through humour and anecdotes. Hence it is regarded as somewhat subversive, but nevertheless it also promotes a contemplative lifestyle as a way of seeking unity with the mysterious principle of nature, namely the *Dao*. The *Chuang-tzu* emphasizes the fact of change or flux, and our futility in resisting it; it glorifies simplicity and spontaneity.

The texts of Lao-tzu and Chuang-tzu influenced later Chinese thinkers, and offered a means for people to rise above human existence and attain immortality: to do this they would have to "steal the secret of Heaven and Earth", that is, seize from nature itself the meaning of the mystery of life.

QUOTE FROM THE *TAO-TE CHING*

The Dao that can be expressed
Is not the eternal Dao.
The name that can be named
Is not the eternal name.
"Non-existence" I call the beginning of Heaven and Earth.
"Existence" I call the mother of individual beings.
Therefore does the direction towards non-existence
Lead to the sight of the miraculous essence,
The direction towards existence
to the sight of spatial limitations.
Both are one in origin
And different only in name.
On its unity it is called the secret.
The secret's still deeper secret
Is the gateway through which all miracles emerge.

Opening verses of the Tao-te Ching

There are many sacred mountains in China; some are associated with all three main Chinese religions, and some are unique to one. Five mountains are generally associated with Daoism: the pattern that the summits form is determined by geomancy. Emperors have paid homage to these sites, and they are also modern pilgrimage destinations. These are Mount Tai, Mount Hua, Mount Song, Mount Heng (in Shanxi), and Mount Heng (in Hunan). Today they continue to be auspicious and attract many pilgrims.

Daoism

MAIN IDEAS AND INFLUENCE

Even though the "three religions" of China (Buddhism, Confucianism, and Daoism) have merged and mixed, there are still some marked differences. In some ways Daoism is the opposite of Confucianism. Confucianism idealizes the perfect man and woman within society – it makes everything in society sacred. Daoism invites people away from society and back to nature: the sacred is in the spontaneous experiences outside normal social patterns. The goal of Confucianism is to become a sage: a wise person who serves society. The goal of Daoism is to become immortal. Daoism calls on ancient traditions of divination, alchemy, and meditation in order to prolong life. If Confucianism is China's ethical guide and teacher of good social behaviours, then Daoism is the magic garden in which the curious children freely play.

The *Dao*

Daoism has little ordering of its beliefs and rituals, and in many ways is ambiguous. Nevertheless a core idea is that Daoists seek unity with the *Dao* – the Ultimate Way. This *Dao* cannot be named, yet Daoists will call on the ancient gods to aid them in their search for immortality. Freedom is a common theme throughout Daoism: freedom from political and social constraints, living fully, and seeking oneness with the *Dao*. The *Dao* might be thought of as the sum total of all that is and all that changes. The *Chuang-tzu* tells us that the *Dao* is "complete, all-embracing, the whole: these are different names for the same reality denoting the One".

Wu-wei: Action Through Non-action

The underlying principle that pervades the universe is the *Dao*. The Daoist texts teach us that we should conform to the *Dao*. Since nature acts spontaneously, we too need spontaneity and naturalness. We do not strive for this: the Way is not something that is to be followed. Instead, paradoxically, we find the *Dao* through *wu-wei*, that is, non-action. By accepting change rather than resisting it; by "going with the flow" rather than fighting against the current, we can live in accord with nature, and hence sees things for what they are. The world that can be named is the world of un-nameable Reality.

Emptiness

"Emptiness" is a theme in Daoism: where there are mountains, there are valleys; water is formless fluidity; a pot is empty, but exists to be filled. It follows that non-action, naturalness, passivity, quietness – these are the ways to inner stillness. Where Confucianism is active, social, and conventional, Daoism is silent, anarchistic, and intuitive: ultimately it is not thought at all.

Daoism's Influence Today

Today Daoism is perhaps one of the world's most widespread religions, and yet the world's most implicit. Many Daoist ideas have been simply woven not only into the very fabric of the Chinese worldview, but into the ideas, social movements, and ideologies of the West. Daoism influenced the counterculture of the 1960s. Author Jack Kerouac, icon of the Beat generation in the 1950s, not only embraced Buddhist ideas, but carried in his back pocket Daoist texts. Lisa, of *The Simpsons*, offers advice to her brother Bart based on ideas from both Zen Buddhism and the *Dao*. Hollywood has produced films shaped by Daoism: *The Karate Kid* (1984, 2010) and *Teenage Ninja Turtles* (1990) are two examples, while films explicitly Daoist with Chinese themes are popular too, such as the Bruce Lee Kung Fu films, as well as *Crouching Tiger, Hidden Dragon* (2000).

A still from *The Karate Kid* (2010). Karate and the martial arts draw on stances of *Tai Chi*, which seeks to cultivate balance, concentration, and relaxation.

FENG SHUI AND TAI CHI

The ancient practice of *feng shui* is based in part on Daoist principles about the natural world. *Feng shui* ("wind and water") is the art of positioning things in order to balance *chi,* the life energy. Originally used to position graves on the sides of hills, some architects and decorators in both the East and the West now use *feng shui* in their designs. For example, the alleged energy patterns of the home will determine what colours might be used: on the shady side of the house, strong reds, oranges, and yellows may be used.

The rapid spread and growth of martial arts schools around the world, and the popularity of *tai chi* exercise is evidence of Daoism's popularity. In *tai chi,* the practitioner is seeking to unify the different parts of the self in flowing and deliberate postures and movements. In the calm and relaxed state of the body, mind, and spirit is found strength and meaning. Books titled with the words "The Tao of…" are too numerous to count. Perhaps they seek to capture the sense of self-fulfilment, peace, quiet, and fullness of living that the Daoist texts suggest is possible. All this is in the service of the pursuit of immortality.

Simply put, whenever the ideals of nourishing life meet a desire for immortality, one can look for hints of Daoism. Although Daoism can be ambiguous and without much seeming order, some structure has emerged during Chinese history: ghosts, demons, and ancestors are all called upon through ritual to aid Daoists in their pursuit of immortality. Those who achieve immortality — supernatural heroes of myth and legend — are in essence gods.

During the New Year holiday, worshippers come to pray and make offerings at Wong Tai Sin Temple in Kowloon, Hong Kong. The temple itself is home to the three Chinese religions: Buddhism; Confucianism; and Daoism.

Confucianism

CONFUCIUS THE MAN

Confucius (c. 551–479 BC) is recognized as a wise teacher, politician, writer, and social philosopher. His teaching and writing has influenced and shaped much of Chinese civilization. "Confucius" is the English form of *K'ung Fu-tzu*, which literally means "Master Kung". Much of what we know of Confucius is a blend of fact and myth from texts written more than 300 years after he died. The court historian Sima Qian (145–85 BC) of the Han dynasty recorded much of what has become the standard story of Confucius's life in *Records of the Grand Historian*.

Shakyamuni Buddha, Confucius, and Lao Tzu, founder of Chinese Taoism, Wang Shu-Ku painting, 18th century.

His Early Life

Confucius was born to a noble family, in the city of Qufu, of the Zhou dynasty state of Lu (c. 1042–249 BC). This is in today's Shandong province. His family fell on bad times, and his childhood was spent in poverty. Sima Qian records that Confucius's birth was an answer to the prayers of his parents. He was probably educated by a Daoist master, learning poetry and music as well as Daoist teachings. By the middle of his life he had gathered some disciples and engaged with the political challenges of the Lu state.

His Exile and Return

When Confucius reached fifty, the Lu duke recognized his abilities and gave him government responsibilities. In his various roles as public servant, Confucius became familiar with the injustices that the nobility imposed on the serfs. While still a government bureaucrat, Confucius challenged this, but some took offence, and he was forced into exile. The theme of exile and suffering is common in religious literature: it is within a small company of disciples that Confucius wandered through the Zhou states looking for a king who might employ him. In this exile, suffering dangers and ridicule, Confucius's ideas took shape. At a close reading, his writings during this time appear to be mere retellings of older Chinese songs and literature. Nevertheless, if not totally original, they are now more meaningfully acted out, and this wisdom takes on flesh in the life of Confucius himself.

Map shows the spread of Confucianism through the Asian world.

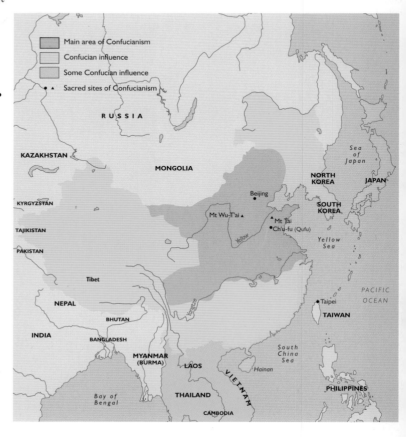

Main area of Confucianism
Confucian influence
Some Confucian influence
• Sacred sites of Confucianism

● SEE ALSO
BUDDHISM PP. 46–53
CHINESE RELIGION PP. 54–55
DAOISM PP. 56–59
JAPANESE RELIGION AND SHINTO PP. 104–105

In 484 BC Confucius returned to the state of Lu and began teaching, editing literary works, and compiling the Lu state court records. The content and quality of these works have elevated him to be the spiritual ancestor of teachers, historians, scholars, and philosophers of Chinese intellectual history.

WRITER AND EDITOR

Confucius is credited as authoring or editing many of the Chinese classics, including the well-known *Analects*. He writes of himself in the *Analects*, "at 15, I set my heart on learning. At 30, I became firm. At 40, I had no more doubts. At 50, I understood heaven's will. At 70, I could follow my heart's desires, without overstepping the line."

Primary school children dress in Confucian costume at the Confucius temple in Nanjing, to celebrate the beginning of school.

The Teacher of Wisdom

Within 100 years or so of his death, Confucius was recognized as a unique figure who should have become a king. Mencius (c. 372–289 BC) said of Confucius, "Ever since man came into this world, there has never been one greater than Confucius." Other disciples followed; for example, in his own writings, Xunzi (c. 312–230 BC) talks of Confucius as a teacher of wisdom.

SAYINGS OF CONFUCIUS

Many of Confucius's sayings have become well known. They are a mixture of spiritual insight, political comment, and good old common sense. Confucius's sayings were worked out in the trauma of exile, and in the daily challenges of political life. Some examples include:

"Forget injuries, never forget kindnesses."

"I hear and I forget. I see and I remember. I do and I understand."

"It does not matter how slowly you go so long as you do not stop."

"To be able under all circumstances to practise five things constitutes perfect virtue: these five things are gravity, generosity of soul, sincerity, earnestness, and kindness."

"When we see men of a contrary character, we should turn inwards and examine ourselves."

Confucianism

KEY IDEAS, TEACHINGS, THE *ANALECTS*

"Confucianism" is a way of living ethically in society that is based largely on the writings and teachings of Confucius, and also subsequent interpretations of his writings. It is sometimes not thought of as a religion at all. While Confucianism is a worldview that shapes the lives of millions of people, it has little to say about the nature of God, for example. Rather than attempting to make sense of ultimate questions, it is more about making sense of everyday life. Some regard it as a humanistic philosophy or an ethical system. Today's Chinese government does not recognize Confucianism as a religion. However, because it does have rituals and rites, and Confucius himself drew on the ancient Chinese idea of heaven, it could be considered a religion of sorts. He declared, "Heaven is the author of the virtue that is in me."

Confucius: An Ethical Teacher

Confucius was critical of the religion of his day, and because of non-stop regional warfare, he wanted to develop a practical ethical way of living so that people could simply get along with each other. So he is best appreciated as a great ethical teacher.

Founders and Leaders

Even though it bears his name, Confucianism cannot really be said to have been founded by Confucius. Later disciples – particularly Mencius (c. 372–289 BC) – compiled and interpreted his work.

Confucianism has no formal hierarchy or priesthood. Neither is there any congregational life. However, in practice, statues and images of Confucius are venerated, and temples have been built to honour him as a deity of learning.

Jen and Li

Confucianism includes the idea of *jen* (virtue, benevolence, humaneness) and *li* (correct manner, protocol, or acts of virtue and goodness). *Jen* and *li* are related, and they are expressed in five relationships:

1. the ruler and his subjects;
2. the parent and child;
3. the husband and wife;
4. the elder brother and the younger;
5. the older and younger friend.

These relationships form the basis of good society. They are expressions of filial piety, and can be extended to ancestors as well.

Confucian Texts

There are five Confucian classics:

1. *Book of History:* a book of history drawing on writings from before the time of Confucius
2. *Book of Songs:* a book of poetry
3. *Book of Changes (I Ching):* a manual of divination and philosophy that is popular in the West today
4. *Rites:* a collection of various rituals
5. *The Spring, Autumn Annals:* a chronological record of the state of Lu.

In addition, there are four books that form the curriculum for Confucian education and that Chinese imperial officers had to be schooled in. These are the *Analects*, *The Doctrine of the Mean*, *The Great Learning*, and *Mencius*.

THE *ANALECTS*

The *Analects* is the most recognizable of Confucian texts. A collection of twenty chapters (or "books"), it is the key source for understanding Confucian ideas. The *Analects* may well consist of some later material added by Confucius's disciples: it was probably written in the years after Confucius's death, and it informs a lot of Chinese literature that followed. Chapter ten of the *Analects* is made up of Confucius's personal observations as a thinker and teacher. This biographical text portrays Confucius as the ideal man or "gentleman". Hence Confucius is the model par excellence of courtliness, decorum, and etiquette.

The *Analects* outlines the four basic concepts of Confucian thought:

1. benevolence, love of humanity, and the virtues of man
2. moderation in all things and harmony with nature
3. filial propriety, duty, and the rules that define good social relationships
4. recognizing the nature of things by giving them their right names.

Rites

Living ethically involves participating in certain rituals known as "rites". These, however, are not acts of worship or prayer, nor do they try to influence the favour of the gods (like making it rain), or save people from evil. Rather, the rites act as a way for the community to bond and integrate as in, for example, the yearly sweeping of graves, the frequent burning of incense at temple sites, and demonstrations of filial piety. This integration is not only on this earth in this life, but also with the deceased ancestors. Underlying this is the idea of balance and harmony: if the rites are not done, then the harmony of the cosmos is compromised and the community is broken.

Education

Because Confucianism is about social ethics – how to live well in society – it follows that education is important. Confucius believed that education was more about building character than gaining knowledge. It was only through the cultivation of self that society could be transformed and kept in unity and harmony. It is not surprising, then, to find Confucian ideals in social philosophy, political philosophy, and the legal system as well.

Actors chanting Confucius' Lunyu, or *Analects*, during the 2008 Beijing Olympic Games opening ceremony.

Confucianism

THE LEGACY IN CHINA

Confucianism can be understood to be "overcoming chaos with character". Another way of saying this might be "What does it mean to be a gentleman?" or "How can I become a wise man?" In early China this was hotly debated, particularly between Daoists and Confucians, but also by those within each of these traditions. This question of how to have good character and live an ethical life extended to the state as well: how can the state be "wise" and facilitate the good character, unity, and wisdom of its people?

Several prominent students followed Confucius. They wrestled with these questions and developed his work. It is well recognized that most of Chinese thinking has been shaped by Confucius, namely that concerning education, politics, social structure, and the economy. Two schools of thinking emerged as "neo-Confucianism" during the Song dynasty (AD 960–1279): the "school of principle" and the "school of mind". Both sought to explore what it means to be a sage. Confucianism spread and influenced the religious worldviews of Korea, Japan, and Vietnam to a degree.

A poster for the Chinese-produced movie, *Confucius*. Starring the popular actor Yun-Fat Chow, it was well received by critics in the West in 2010.

The Family

Much in Confucianism is about harmony: personal, social, and political spheres are intertwined. In a sense even family and state are one and the same: training to be a sage family head is essentially the same as being a wise head of state. One Confucian scholar talked of the state as being a family. Harmony is understood to be a balance of duty to family with duty to strangers, a balance between good and bad, between this world and the next, between humility and power. One is to act in ways that always seek to bring harmony within these apparent paradoxes.

Heaven

Even though Confucianism is "earthly", that is, about living life well on earth, the idea of heaven is woven through it. Confucius implied that heaven was a supreme deity of sorts. Mencius, another important Confucian thinker, was more ambivalent. The philosopher Hsun-tzu was more explicitly pantheistic: he believed heaven is the universe itself. But heaven was not considered as a reward for good behaviour when one dies or a place to which one goes: goodness was its own reward.

Successors to Confucius

MENCIUS (372–289 BC)

Although living in a time of huge social upheaval in China, Mencius nonetheless promoted the idea that humankind is essentially good. This goodness is derived from the idea that humans are connected to the "Way of Heaven". Expanding on the idea of *jen/ren* (being human through looking out for others, or simply "human-ness"), Mencius believed a certain intuitive mysticism can lead to the joy of being an enlightened sage. This idealism also implied that rulers should seek the best for their people.

HSUN-TZU (312–238 BC)

Contrary to the idealism of Mencius, Hsun-tzu was a realist, and he suggested that humanity was basically selfish. Nevertheless, improvement could be made through learning. Hsun-tzu promoted rationalism over superstition; he argued for tradition and ritual action, believing that these could transform the human heart. Hsun-tzu believed that if one does not have rituals as the core of daily living, then the teachings of Confucius and Mencius would become impossible to keep.

CHU HSI (AD 1130–1200)

Known as a "neo-Confucian", Chu Hsi drew on Daoist and Buddhist ideas as well as Confucian ones. He promoted meditation on and for the Confucian ideals of *jen/ren*. If one wanted to become an ideal sage, then ethics and meditation went hand in hand. This self-cultivation and "examination of all things" was important, and this happened gradually. One should attempt to know oneself (through meditation), in order to perfect one's original nature (which is good). Chu Hsi's interpretation of Confucianism became the norm for all bureaucrats in the Chinese civil service from the 1300s to the 1900s, who could gain their positions only after extensive examinations.

WANG YANG-MING (AD 1472–1529)

In the neo-Confucian school, Wang Yang-ming agreed with his predecessors that the goal of life was sagehood, but Wang Yang-ming rejected Chu Hsi's gradual meditative approach. He believed that only an enlightened experience of unity of one's mind with the Dao – the ultimate mind/way – would be a sufficient way of achieving sagehood.

Marching crowds wave red banners and posters of Mao during the 1967 Cultural Revolution.

> ## CONFUCIUS'S "GOLDEN RULE"
>
> *Do not inflict on others what you yourself would not wish done to you.*
>
> **Analects 15:24**

Confucianism and the Challenges of the Twentieth Century

Because of its strong sense of tradition and its hierarchical nature, Confucianism has been criticized for hindering democracy, subjugating women, and stifling economic development. For example, in Confucianism the ideal society should be ruled by an autocratic sage; that is, the elite should rule the common people. The ideal society is one of harmony and peace. Confucianism does not promote human rights like freedom of speech.

Today's Chinese government, while ideologically Communist, has been able to find a way of holding on to Confucian values. "Harmony" of the state has been redefined; there is a recognition that to proceed into the future, one has to maintain social order and continuity. Communism levels everyone: all are to act with propriety. Thus today's government justifies its actions by appealing to Confucianism.

Strong economic development of China and Taiwan is explained in Confucian terms as well: a strong economy requires a strong state, good education, and model families. Nevertheless, for women, the filial piety as expressed in the strong father–son relationship has been a problem. To be an ideal woman in Confucian terms, the woman should look after the family and be obedient to her husband. Marriage represents harmony and longevity, whereas modern couples may prefer other goals, such as mutuality and happiness.

Judaism

HISTORICAL FOUNDATIONS AND OVERVIEW

Judaism is the religion of the Jewish people, but not all Jews are active participants in Judaism. The prophet Moses is the historical focal point. Nevertheless, Judaism has older roots in Abraham, whom many consider to be the "father of the Jewish people": the Jews as an ethnic group are descendants of Abraham and claim that God gave them the "Promised Land", that is, an area of land that is slightly larger than the current land area of modern Israel. The exodus, which is a defining event that shaped the Jews' identity, was led by Moses: it was a journey out of slavery in Egypt to the Promised Land, during which Moses received God's Law for his people.

Judaism has changed considerably over its approximately 3,000-year history. Today, Judaism is one of the smallest of the world religions, and at first glance, seems confined merely to the modern state of Israel. Israel's population is around 8 million, and about 75 per cent of these are Jews in the broadest definition of the word. Worldwide, however, there are around 14 million Jews. This is testimony to the fact that they have often been dispersed by the rise and fall of empires. Many Jews then left and found new homes among the nations of the world.

Judaism Takes Shape

Judaism as we know it today really started to take shape after the first destruction of the Jerusalem Temple in 586 BC. While exiled in Babylon, the Jews were cut off from their holy sites, particularly the Temple of Jerusalem; as a result, the Jews had to invent a "mobile" religion. Religious rituals could no longer be performed by priests at the Jerusalem Temple; the Hebrew Scriptures had to be written down and made more widely available to exiles; worship had to take on new forms – singing, teaching, Scripture reading – in new religious locations called synagogues. The sacrificial system, so central to worship at the Temple in Jerusalem, could not be done in synagogues in Babylon.

With the return of the Jews from exile in Persia to Jerusalem (in several waves between 538 and 433 BC), the Jews brought back these new forms of worship. The Temple underwent a series of rebuilds, right into the reign of the Roman king Herod (c. 74 BC – AD 4). This Temple was destroyed in AD 70, and the Jews again dispersed to other lands.

Left: The Arch of Titus is a triumphal structure located on the Via Sacra, Rome. It was constructed by Emperor Domitian c. AD 82 to commemorate the sacking of Jerusalem and features a depiction of the Roman troops carrying off the *menorah* (candlestick).
Right: Celebration of Simchat Torah, the end of Sukkot, at the Wailing Wall, Jerusalem. Jews dance with the Torah as a symbol that the yearly reading cycle is at an end, and they prepare to start the cycle once more.

Patriarchy and the Covenant

. . . .

Patriarchs (the "fathers") other than Abraham and Moses also play a significant role in Judaism, and their stories are found in the first five books of the Hebrew Scriptures – the "books of Moses" or the "Pentateuch". These are also the first five books of the Christian Bible. The covenant plays a central role in Judaism: this covenant is between God and the patriarchs, taking full expression during Moses' leadership. Nevertheless, the covenant with Noah, for example, is for the Gentiles (non-Jews) as well.

A Way of Life

. . . .

With the idea of covenant being central, it can be said that Judaism focuses on how to live in this world: how to live according to what God expects of his chosen people, here and now. Hence ritual and ethics dominate Judaism.

TORAH

The Torah is the name of the first five books of the Jewish Scriptures, usually attributed to Moses. In a broader sense, Torah also means "that which is written", and can include those oral traditions handed down and now embodied as Talmud (from the third century AD) and Midrash (an ongoing interpretive tradition).

SYNAGOGUE

"Synagogue" is a Greek term, capturing the Hebrew idea of "assembly" or, more precisely, a "house of prayer". It is thought that their formation was a response to the Babylonian captivity (sixth century BC): in other words, the exiles joined together in prayer in "assemblies" in Babylon, as they no longer had access to the Temple in Jerusalem. The synagogue gave Judaism the opportunity to become "portable" – diaspora Jews could assemble in a sanctified space that represented the Temple. Perhaps because of this need for

social identity and cohesion, a synagogue today often has the additional function of being a community centre.

TEMPLE

Built on Mount Zion (later known as the "Temple Mount") in Jerusalem, the Temple was viewed as being the dwelling place of God's name, or his "footstool". The Temple is in continuity with the Tabernacle, which was the portable tent used by the Israelites when they left captivity in Egypt (variously dated between 1400 and 1200 BC). Although it was King David's desire to build the Temple, it was his son Solomon who managed to construct the "First Temple" in the tenth century BC. It was pillaged during the Assyrian crisis (c. 700 BC), then totally destroyed during the Babylonian conflict in 586 BC. The Second Temple was rebuilt by Ezra and returned exiles, and completed about 517 BC, then greatly enhanced by Herod the Great (d. 4 BC). It was finally destroyed by the Romans in AD 70. Today, on the mount on which the

Temple once stood, stands the Al Aqsa mosque. The Western (or Wailing) Wall, standing at the foot of the Temple Mount, is the only part of Herod's temple that is still in existence. It is considered to be one of the most sacred sites of Judaism.

COVENANT

Judaism is founded on a covenant that stipulates the nature of the relationship between God and the Israelites. The covenant assured the Israelites of God's blessing, in return for their obedience. The covenant is interpreted variously throughout Israel's history: we can talk of the covenant of Adam, Noah, Abraham, Moses, David, the priestly covenant, and even a promised new covenant. Various symbols associated with the covenant are widely known: Noah's rainbow and circumcision (stipulated by Moses) are just two examples.

Judaism

THE PATRIARCH, MOSES

Judaism regards Moses as the first and greatest prophet. After the Egyptian pharaoh had invited Jacob and his sons to make their home in Egypt, subsequent pharaohs realized Jacob's descendants had become too numerous, and so forced them into slavery. The date of this is in the late second millennium BC. This is recorded in the book of Genesis, the first book in the Jewish Torah and the Christian Old Testament. The people cried out to God in their slavery, and God answered by causing Moses to be born. Moses barely survived childhood, being set afloat in a cane basket on the River Nile to avoid the execution of all Hebrew male babies. Pharaoh's daughter found the baby Moses in the basket beside the Nile, took him in, and raised him as her own. When Moses as a grown man committed murder, he escaped into exile in Midian, where he married and was a shepherd for forty years. It is during this time that he encountered the call of God in a burning bush, and because of this returned to Egypt with the mission to free the Hebrews from their slavery. All of this is recorded in the book of Exodus, the second book of the Torah.

Passover

God's power over the Egyptian gods was demonstrated in the ten plagues: the tenth plague – where the Egyptian firstborn died but the spirit of the Lord "passed over" the homes of the Israelites, thus sparing their children – is celebrated today in the festival of Passover. Moses led the Hebrews and others – approximately 2 million – out of Egypt, parting the *yam suph* – the Sea of Reeds (wrongly translated as the "Red Sea") on the way. As they wandered in the Sinai Desert for forty years, God shaped these exiles into a nation under Moses' leadership.

God's Covenant

Moses received the Ten Commandments from God on Mount Sinai, where God entered into covenant with the people. God promised to the people love and care, demonstrated as a place to live (land), a reputation (a name), and descendants. This promise was conditional on their obedience to God. Moses handed over leadership to Joshua and was not able to enter the Promised Land (in the area of modern Israel/Palestine) due to disobedience. He died on its borders.

Moses and the Law

In Judaism, Moses is associated with the Law (the Ten Commandments and other laws), covenant, and Passover. He is also regarded as a prophet – one to whom God revealed himself, and who in turn shares God's message with the people. In contrast to the founders of other religions, Moses is not thought of as a god himself and is not glorified in any sense.

A family celebrates Seder. Before Seder begins, the celebrants are guided through the service by means of a narrative called the "Haggadah", from which everybody reads.

THE TEN COMMANDMENTS

The Ten Commandments (or "Ten words", or Decalogue) given to Moses by God, appears in two versions in the Bible: Exodus 20 and Deuteronomy 5. They are readily abbreviated into point form and sometimes placed as plaques on synagogue and church walls.

1	You shall have no other gods before me
2	You shall not make for yourselves any graven image
3	You shall not take the name of the Lord your God in vain
4	Remember the Sabbath day and keep it holy
5	Honour your father and your mother
6	You shall not murder
7	You shall not commit adultery
8	You shall not steal
9	You shall not bear false witness against your neighbour
10	You shall not covet anything that is your neighbour's

The Books of Moses

The "five books of Moses" are authoritative in Judaism and are known collectively as the Torah. In the Christian Bible, they are the first five books of the Old Testament.

GENESIS

This, the first book in the Torah, narrates the creation of the world. It also includes the stories of the patriarchs (Abraham, Noah, Isaac, Jacob, and Joseph) and explains God's first covenants. The story of Noah and the rainbow – the sign of the covenant – is in Genesis.

EXODUS

This book tells the story of Moses, from his birth to his leadership of the escape from Egypt and his wanderings in the desert. It explains how God forms the people into one nation and makes a covenant with them.

LEVITICUS

This book is comprised mainly of ritual laws and worship patterns – namely those to do with animal sacrifices – in which the priests (Levites) were to lead the people.

NUMBERS

A census of the people, this book also reiterates the laws and festivals.

DEUTERONOMY

The last of the "Five Books", Deuteronomy includes a collection of sermons preached by Moses before the people entered the Promised Land, reminding them of God's covenant and their responsibilities.

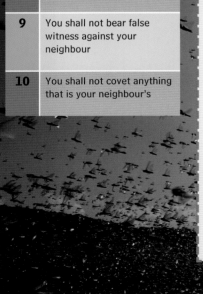

THE TEN PLAGUES

In order to show God's dominance over the Egyptian gods and persuade Pharaoh to release the Israelites from slavery, God brought ten plagues upon the Egyptians. The tenth and final plague led to the Israelites' release (see Exodus 5–12).

The first plague – river water turned to blood	The sixth plague – boils
The second plague – frogs	The seventh plague – hail
The third plague – gnats	The eighth plague – locusts
The fourth plague – flies	The ninth plague – darkness
The fifth plague – death of livestock	The tenth plague – death of the firstborn

Judaism

BELIEF

Monotheism – the belief in one God – is perhaps the defining characteristic of Judaism. For Jews, God is sovereign creator, ruler, sustainer, provider, and saviour. God is long-suffering and merciful, just yet loving. God is all-knowing and all-powerful, and exists eternally. The book of Genesis narrates God's creation of the world beginning with the making of heaven and earth and ending with the creation of humans.

This same God revealed himself to Moses in a burning bush at Mount Sinai by the name I AM (Exodus 3:14). This has been very difficult to translate. In English it sometimes appears as the four-lettered "YHWH". This is God's holy name, and a Jew will not pronounce, write, or say it. It is the covenant name for God with his people. The covenant is sourced from God's character of goodness: it is a moral covenant that defines sin – what an offence to God looks like – as well as forgiveness.

SHEMA

The word "Shema" translates to "Hear, O Israel" and is the name of a prayer that Jews recite at morning and evening prayer services. It is both a prayer and a declaration of faith. The prayer affirms the central Jewish belief in one God. It is best known by its opening line in the book of Deuteronomy:

"Hear, O Israel: The Lord our God, the Lord is one. Love the Lord your God with all your heart and with all your soul and with all your strength" (Deuteronomy 6:4–5).

Law

In Judaism, Law is important. This is not "law" in the sense of the state judicial system, but rather the ritual worship patterns and community principles laid down in the five books of Moses, as well as the wider interpretation of that Law. At the core it is the Ten Commandments, written on stone tablets by the "finger of God" and given to Moses on Mount Sinai (Exodus 20 and Deuteronomy 5). These were placed in the ark of the covenant in the Holy of Holies in the Temple in Jerusalem, but now they are lost to antiquity. A total of 613 laws exist in supplementary material. Some Jews literally tie the laws to their arms and forehead in small boxes at times of worship. The prophetic tradition sought to interpret and call people back to the essence of the Law. For example, the prophet Micah calls on the people to "act justly and to love mercy and to walk humbly with God" (Micah 6:8). The teacher Rabbi Hillel the Elder (c. 110 BC–AD 10) summarized the Law: "what is hateful to you do not do to your neighbour. The rest is commentary. Go and learn it" (*Shabbat* 31a).

Talmud

The Talmud is a core text of Judaism. "Talmud" means instruction or learning based on the teaching of the rabbis (teachers). It is in the form of discussions between rabbis about Jewish law, ethics, customs, history, and philosophy. It has two components: the *Mishnah* (opinions and debates on the law, c. AD 200) and the *Gemara* (further commentaries on the *Mishnah*, c. AD 500).

MAIMONIDES AND THE THIRTEEN PRINCIPLES OF FAITH

Moses Maimonides (c. 1135–1204) is acknowledged as perhaps Judaism's greatest philosopher, writing prolifically on Jewish law and ethics. He is widely considered to be the founder of Jewish scholarship, and his most well-known book is *The Guide to the Perplexed*. One of his greatest contributions to Jewish belief was his formulation of the "thirteen principles of faith", derived from the Torah. Today, these principles are widely held as the basic tenets of Judaism.

Eretz (the Land)

Israel, approximating the Promised Land spoken of in the books of Moses, has always held a high place in Jewish religious and political life. The Scriptures clearly lay out its boundaries, but they have been variously interpreted over the generations. The land is part of the covenantal agreement between God and the Jewish people, and reached its most expansive borders in the reign of King Solomon (c. 970–931 BC).

Jerusalem

The city of Jerusalem has always been the centre of Judaism, although today full and free access to holy sites in Jerusalem for Jews is a problem. The Temple site in Jerusalem is associated with Mount Moriah, where Abraham almost offered his son Isaac as a sacrifice. Around 1000 BC, King David captured Salem – a term with connotations of "peace" and "safety"

– and made it into his religious and political capital, Jerusalem. Zion is another name for the Temple Mount specifically and the Jerusalem area more generally. Jerusalem was sacked in 586 BC, was rebuilt, and then was again overrun in AD 70. It was razed completely in AD 135 following the Bar Kochba revolt against the Romans. Nevertheless, a Jewish population has always lived in or near Jerusalem. In the twentieth century – in light of the Holocaust and the desire for a homeland – Jerusalem city again became the focus of the hopes and aspirations of Judaism. It is now contested space, with both Christians and Muslims wanting access to it.

Orthodox Jews praying in front of the Western Wall, Jerusalem. The Wall, probably dating from restoration work done by Herod the Great (1st century BC), has become representative of the hopes and dreams of many Jews.

Judaism

RITUAL AND ACTION

In Judaism ritual and action play a central role. Because of this, we can talk about an "observant" or "practising" Jew. Ritual is *mitzvot*, a holy commandment. *Mitzvot* includes worship acts, and makes ordinary routines holy: eating, for instance, is transformed by rules of *kosher*. Practising Jews eat certain things in certain ways because of religious truths.

The Law is lived out in *halakha*. These rules, derived from the Scriptures and the teaching of the rabbis, cover all the actions of daily life from morning to night. Roles are clearly defined and taught from generation to generation. Another way of understanding this is to recognize Judaism as a religion of ethics, in which love for God is shown through how people live their lives.

Because law and ethics are central, it follows that Judaism has strong ideals of justice. All people are equal before God's law. Hence charity and giving are ritualized as tithe (10 per cent of income). Widows, orphans, and the poor are identified as needy. The year of Jubilee (every fiftieth year) ideally proclaims liberty for the land and slaves (Leviticus 25:10), although there is little evidence that this has been regularly celebrated. The Talmud has many laws regarding justice.

Shabbat

A unique routine of Judaism is *Shabbat*, a rest day on the seventh day of the week. *Shabbat* is from sundown on Friday to sundown on Saturday. It represents the order of creation (see Genesis 1–2:3), and the command in Exodus not to work at all (Exodus 16:29): a faithful Jew must rest completely on that one day.

Study and Learning

Judaism is a religion "of the book". Jews' reverence for the Torah means they study it rigorously. Study is a religiously significant event. The authority of the *rabbi* (teacher) is closely linked to his knowledge of the religious Law, rather than to priestly status or personality. Some might think that Judaism's priority for study and learning leads to a highly rationalized religion, a religion "of the head". (Magic and superstition, for example, are not tolerated.) This learning and study leads to highly developed ethical systems and codes of behaviour.

Kosher

Literally meaning "prepared", *kosher* refers to various rules regarding eating and food preparation. Certain meats are not allowed, for example, and slaughtering of animals must be done in a special way. Blood is to be totally removed, as it represents the life given by God. There are various other rules associated with the preparation and eating of dairy foods as well. The idea is these rules make the act of eating holy: it is a sacred event, done in recognition of God's provision. *Kosher* is also a religious boundary marker; it is a public way of expressing community identity.

The nine-branch *menorah* (candlestick) is used at the festival of Hanukkah to remember the Temple of Jerusalem. Here, large crowds watch the lighting of the National Menorah on the Ellipse near the White House in Washington, USA.

Family and Relationship Purity

Various rules and purity rituals shape the relationship between husband and wife. Men are obliged to perform the regulations of the Commandments, but women are not required to do these. Men are expected, for example, to pray three times a day. However, these regulations, among others, are being openly challenged within Judaism, and women are taking on roles – including study and prayer – that have been men's roles in the past.

JEWISH LIFE CYCLE CELEBRATIONS

Circumcision (B'rit milah)
Bar/bat mitzvah
Wedding
Death/burial/mourning

Diagram shows the Jewish festivals and holy days. The Jewish calendar is based on both lunar and solar cycles. The religious year and the calendar year can vary. There is also some variation in which festivals are celebrated by which sects.

Purim
Passover
Unleavened Bread
Second Passover
Feast of Weeks or Shavuot (Pentecost)

Adar 12 · Nisan 1 · Shevat 11 · Iyar 2 · Tevet 10 · Sivan 3 · Kislev 9 · Tammuz 4 · Heshvan 8 · Av 5 · Tishri 7 · Elul 6

Mar · Feb · Jan · Apr · May · Dec · Jun · Nov · Jul · Oct · Sep · Aug

Hanukkah

Last Great Day
Feast of Booths or Tabernacles (Succot)
Day of Atonement (Yom Kippur)
Trumpets
New Year (Rosh Ha-Shanah)

A rabbi reads the Torah before the Synagogue of the Premishlan congregation on Purim holiday, Israel.

73

Judaism

MODERN JUDAISM AND THE STATE

Beginning with the Babylonian exile, the Jewish people have lived out a long history of exile from, and return to, the Promised Land. With rising nationalism across Europe in the nineteenth century, together with the world wars of the twentieth century (including Hitler's extermination of nearly a third of the global Jewish population), the Jews' story of exile and return became embodied in a movement called Zionism, led by Theodor Herzl (1860–1904). Herzl politicized the possibilities of a homeland state. Hence modern Israel was founded in 1948, but not without a struggle. Jerusalem was divided under siege by Arab armies. In the Six Day War of 1967, Jews regained the eastern sector and annexed it. Technically, Jerusalem is the capital of Israel, with all government departments located there. Due to ongoing disputes over the status of the Palestinian people, however, the international community has not recognized Jerusalem as the capital.

The state of Israel became a home for the displaced Jews after the Second World War. This new Israel opened its doors wide. The Law of Return declared that any Jew had the right to become a citizen of Israel, and the new nation was populated very rapidly.

Today, Israel's official religion is Judaism of the Orthodox form. The state celebrates Judaism's festivals, and Jewish religious symbols are on government buildings. Although the state recognizes a number of religious groups, Jews make up around 75 per cent of the population. The number of Jews in America is comparable to the number of Jews in Israel.

Modern Judaism

During the twentieth century, the definition of "Jew" shifted. This is called the Emancipation. In their diaspora communities in Europe, Jews were tight communities – "a nation within a nation" – but now a Jew had the freedom to be "a citizen of the Mosaic faith". The governments of host nations allowed the Jews to integrate better into society. Hence the question of what is "essential" to Judaism became important, especially if ritual and keeping to Torah were compromised by diaspora Jews.

Reform Judaism

Reform Judaism focuses on the ethical core – how to live out morality and justice, rather than strictly keeping to the teachings of Moses and the rabbis. Reform Judaism has been shaped by the changes the Jewish community in Germany experienced in the eighteenth century. Perhaps due to the growing influence of science, German rabbi Abraham Geiger (1810–74) considered that the Torah could not be regarded as factual. Therefore doctrinal adjustments should be encouraged, and various regulations could be relaxed or done away with. Worship could be shifted from *Shabbat* to Sunday, and new worship forms could be introduced. Consequently, Reform Judaism is considered the most progressive branch of Judaism. For Reform Jews, Torah is meaningful only for religious understanding, not because it came from God.

Orthodox Judaism

Orthodox Judaism seeks to live out the religious and legal codes upon which Judaism was founded. Orthodox Judaism has been influenced by the Eastern European Jewish community of the nineteenth century which found comfort and meaning in the strict adherence to tradition. Orthodox Jews emphasize submission to Torah, which came from God and is therefore completely authoritative. Nevertheless, Rabbi Hirsch (1808–88) and others encouraged Orthodox Jews to go out into the secular world – for example, by going to university – as long as they continued to comply to Torah.

Other Movements

Reconstructionist Judaism was developed by Mordecai Kaplan (1881–1983) in New York, and rejects the idea that the Jews are God's chosen people. Reconstructionist Jews speak of God as the highest ethical ideal, reject the supernatural, and embrace evolution. Humanistic Judaism, originating in 1963 in Detroit, celebrates Jewish culture and individualism, but without God. Prayer and study of Torah are rejected. For the Humanists, Judaism is about "doing good without God".

A modern-day Hasidic Jew.

Central Synagogue in Manhattan, New York, USA.

Conservative Judaism

Conservative Judaism sees Judaism as the collective conscience of Israel. This allows for keeping to tradition, while also permitting flexibility in adapting to new social challenges. For European Jews, it was a priority to preserve the fundamentals of the tradition. In America, the scholar and rabbi Solomon Schechter (1847–1915) appealed for commitment to tradition, but allowed some adaptations within the American context.

HASIDISM AND KABBALAH

Hasidism and Kabbalah are both mystical forms of Judaism. Hasidism arose in Poland in the eighteenth century and emphasizes God's mercy, which is celebrated in music and dance, while Kabbalah draws on a mix of ancient wisdom and hidden knowledge traditions. Both movements cultivate personal spirituality, perhaps as a reaction against the perceived dryness of Judaism's emphasis on study. Kabbalah overlaps with Esoterica, a strand of New Age practice which emphasizes hidden knowledge. Celebrities such as Madonna, David Beckham, Demi Moore, and Britney Spears have all been associated with Kabbalah at one time.

Christianity

THE CENTRALITY OF JESUS

The word "Christianity" comes from the Greek *christos*, which means "anointed one". The translation of the Hebrew word "messiah", *christos* (Christ) is a title given to the historical person Jesus: in other words, he is Jesus (the) Christ, that is, the anointed one (of God).

Christianity started in a Jewish context during the Roman empire. The Gregorian calendar used throughout the world splits history according to the life of Jesus Christ: "BC" is literally "before Christ", and "AD" is for the Latin *anno domini* ("in the year of our Lord"), from the alleged birthdate of Jesus Christ.

Christianity is the world's largest religion (about 32 per cent of the globe): it is the most widely spread and ethnically diverse religion. Christianity is a religion that embraces translation: it has no one holy language. There are over 35,000 different Christian denominations; however, all have the person of Jesus Christ as central.

How Do We Know about Jesus?

The life of Jesus is recorded in the Bible. The Bible has two parts: the Old Testament and the New Testament. Jesus' life is specifically recorded in four Gospels written by Matthew, a former tax collector who became an apostle, or messenger, of Jesus; Mark, a follower of the apostle Peter; Luke, a doctor also credited with writing the New Testament book of Acts; and John, a close disciple of Jesus. These are the first four books of the New Testament. The rest of the New Testament interprets the life and teachings of Jesus for the new Christians in light of their experience of him, and offers a rethinking of the prophecies about Jesus from the Old Testament. The New Testament records both Jesus' earthly life and his ongoing resurrected presence in the world.

Jesus' Life

It is understood Jesus was born supernaturally of a young Jewish virgin called Mary. Her fiancé Joseph wanted to break the engagement, but both were visited by angels to assure them of the future importance of this baby. The Gospel of Luke tells of an angel giving Mary news that she would give birth to the Son of the Most High. Jesus was born in Bethlehem (celebrated in the festival of Christmas), but his family was from Nazareth, where Joseph was a carpenter. We can assume Jesus grew up as Joseph's apprentice, but at around the age of thirty he took up an itinerant teaching role around Lake Galilee in the north of Israel, based in Capernaum.

Jesus' Message

Jesus taught about "the kingdom of God". This rule of God was breaking into history in his own person: hence, Jesus preached that "the time has come", the "kingdom of God is near" and people should "repent" and "believe the good news". The Gospel of Mark for example, uses all this language quite explicitly. The Gospel of Matthew uses the equivalent phrase "kingdom of heaven". Jesus' ministry was accompanied by "signs of the kingdom", that is, miracles. Jesus taught using parables – similes and metaphors from everyday life – to illustrate how this reign of God would work out. Because Jesus implicitly claimed to be divine, the Jewish authorities took offence and manipulated events so that Jesus was crucified in Jerusalem – hung on a Roman cross.

Jesus' Resurrection

A unique sequence of events then follows this execution. The Gospels say that on the third day after the crucifixion, Jesus came back to life (was resurrected) as a new type of living being. All four Gospels record this. The eyewitnesses to this event,

Panel of the triptych in the Uffizi, Florence, depicting the Ascension, by Andrea Mantegna (1431–1506).

How Jesus "Fits" in the Bible

Jesus was a Jew, and Christianity is rooted in Jewish beliefs about the coming of God in person to be with his people. Particularly in the latter part of the Old Testament, this "coming of God" was named as a saviour called "messiah". While Jews reject Jesus as the messiah foretold in the Old Testament, Christians believe that he is, in fact, the messiah.

One of the first tasks of the new Christians was to re-read the Jewish Scriptures (that is, the Old Testament) in light of Jesus' resurrection. They had to work out how to believe in the one God of Judaism but also recognize Jesus' extraordinary claims (the Gospel of John, for example, records Jesus as saying, "I and the Father are one"). The prophets of the Old Testament (particularly Isaiah) had made some remarkable statements that these new Christians now understood to be predictions of a coming messiah, the "anointed one" of God. Christians believe that the God of creation and history, who revealed himself to Israel's patriarchs, the prophets, and the people of Israel more generally, had shown up in person as Jesus, limited by time and space and history. Because of this, the apostle Paul argues in his letters to the first churches in the first century AD (which can be found in the New Testament) that God had created all things through Jesus Christ to begin with, and was now bringing all things together through Jesus Christ.

Paul and the other writers of the New Testament interpret Jesus' crucifixion as a redemptive event. Jesus, as a human sacrifice, died for the sins of the world; in effect God sacrificed his own son, as the embodiment of human sin, so that humanity may be free from the power of sin. This rule of God had started with Jesus Christ, and would come to completion when he returns to bring in the full and final reign of God as king at the end of this present age.

who discovered his empty tomb, were personally so transformed that they enthusiastically spread the news of the resurrection; the number of new Christians boomed. In their minds, this resurrection was so convincing that it confirmed everything that Jesus had taught and modelled: the reign of God had truly broken into history. Jesus promised to continue to be with this growing number of disciples "to the very end of the age" (Matthew 28:20). He then departed from them a final time (the ascension), but gave them power through his Holy Spirit. Today's Christians in all their diversity continue to experience the empowering presence of the resurrected Jesus Christ.

A man who said the sort of things Jesus said would not be a great moral teacher. He would either be a lunatic – on a level with the man who says he is a poached egg – or else he would be the Devil of Hell. You must make your choice. Either this man was, and is, the Son of God: or else a madman or something worse. You can shut Him up for a fool, you can spit at Him and kill Him as a demon; or you can fall at His feet and call Him Lord and God. But let us not come with any patronizing nonsense about His being a great human teacher. He has not left that open to us. He did not intend to.

C. S. Lewis, Mere Christianity

Christianity

ITS ESTABLISHMENT AND SHAPE

Jesus chose twelve disciples (from the Latin *discipulus*, meaning "a learner"), of whom three were close friends (Peter, James, and John). The Gospels also record a wider group that includes women. The fifth book of the New Testament, Acts of the Apostles, tells of how the early church grew: convinced of the resurrection, thousands "were added to their number" (Acts 2:41). Perhaps the most dramatic conversion was that of Saul of Tarsus, whose name changed to Paul following an encounter with the resurrected Jesus on the road to Damascus (Acts 9): he was responsible for much of the spread of the church around the Mediterranean, and the writing of the New Testament (his letters to those churches).

Emperor Constantine bestows the primacy of the Church and the rule over the West on his contemporary pope, Sylvester (314–35).

Detail of a 12th-century mosaic depicting the apostles Matthew, John, Andrew, and Peter.

The Early Church and its Councils

Originally a sect of Judaism, these first Christians had to recognize that Jesus' teaching, death, and resurrection were for the whole world, not just the Jews. They hammered this out at the Council of Jerusalem (c. AD 50), recorded in Acts 15. Worship routines changed: followers met on Sundays, regularly celebrated communion with bread and wine, sang songs, and listened to teaching. On the whole, they refused to bow down to the Roman Caesar, which cost many of them their lives. Much debate followed about right belief, particularly over the nature of Jesus Christ – in what

way could he have been both God and man at the same time? This was resolved eventually at the Council of Chalcedon (AD 451) with the statement that "Jesus Christ was fully God and fully man" – with no further comment or explanation.

Following the Roman emperor Constantine's (c. AD 272–337) conversion to Christianity in AD 312, Christian worship was legalized; prior to this, Christians had been persecuted for their beliefs. It was from this time that the building of churches began and Western Christianity became centred in Rome. With the close ties of church and state, Christendom – literally the "domain of Christ" – existed as an idea and a reality in Europe until the Reformation of the sixteenth century. The key question was: how does one form a Christian society and state?

Movement East

Meanwhile, in the East, due mainly to persecution, the church spread into modern-day Iraq, but its core ideas were slightly different to those of the Western (that is, Roman) church. Moving along the trade route we now call the Silk Road, Christians formed many thriving communities as far east as China by AD 635. This so-called Eastern expression of Christianity fitted roughly in a more general movement now called Orthodox Christianity. Various sects within Orthodox Christianity quickly established themselves outside Roman influence in such places as Egypt, Ethiopia, Armenia, and Syria. The apostle Thomas, for example, was probably the first to take Christianity to India, as early as – by some accounts – AD 52.

The Reformation

The European Reformation of the sixteenth century brought together discontent that had been murmuring for years, and had shown itself in various reform movements. It was Martin Luther (1483–1546), however, who ignited the Reformation, when he nailed his ninety-five theses – propositions he wanted debated in the church – to the castle door at Wittenberg in Germany. The Reformation made good use of the new moveable type in printing: teaching and propaganda could be spread at speeds not experienced before, and, combined with an uprising of the peasants, the social fabric of Europe was changed forever, as was the very structure, beliefs, and worship patterns of the church.

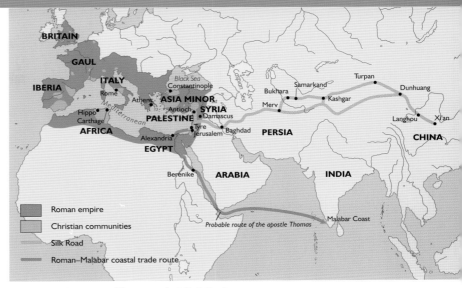

Map shows the far-reaching spread of Christianity.

THREE MAJOR GROUPS WITHIN CHRISTIANITY

There are three main traditions within Christianity. They agree on the basic tenets of the faith regarding Jesus but differ significantly enough on other points to warrant a distinct group.

- The Orthodox churches are located mainly in Russia, eastern Europe, the Middle East, and North Africa, but have also spread due to migration. There are 260–300 million Orthodox Christians worldwide.

- The Roman Catholic Church, with the pope as its head, is based in the Vatican City in Rome. There are about 1 billion (1,000 million) Roman Catholics worldwide.

- The Protestant churches are those that "protested" against Rome in the sixteenth century, but continued to divide and reform themselves into many denominations, some of which were associated with national expressions (Lutherans in Germany, Anglicans in England, and Presbyterians in Scotland, for example). There are around 800 million Protestants.

AUTHORITY IN THE CHURCH

The three main Christian groups have different understandings of spiritual authority.

THE ORTHODOX CHURCH: THE SEVEN CHURCH COUNCILS

In the Western church, that is, the church under the influence of Rome, leaders met periodically in full councils, usually under the patronage of the Roman emperor. These councils met to sort out heresies that had arisen, usually around the nature of Jesus Christ. The findings of these seven councils – understood to have been guided by the Holy Spirit – are now the chief authority of the Orthodox Church.

The seven councils were:

- 325 Nicea
- 381 Constantinople
- 431 Ephesus
- 451 Chalcedon
- 553 Constantinople
- 680 Constantinople
- 787 Nicea

ROME AND THE SUCCESSION OF THE APOSTLE PETER

The Roman Catholic Church understands its authority as derived from a particular reading of Matthew 16:16–20, understanding the disciple Peter to be the "rock" on which the church would be built. The popes are in a line of spiritual succession from Peter, who was the "first bishop" of Rome. It is chiefly the popes and church authorities who interpret Christian life and faith, guided by the Holy Spirit.

PROTESTANTS: THE BIBLE ALONE

There are thousands of Protestant sects and denominations, but they are all "protestant" in as much as they have roots in the sixteenth-century Reformation. Authority is generally understood to be from the Bible, studied and interpreted using literary analysis, but also relying on the ongoing guidance of the Holy Spirit. Protestants read Matthew 16:16–20 not as giving authority to Peter as a person, but to Peter's confession: "You are the Messiah, the Son of the living God." In other words, the church is all those people who make this same confession.

Christianity

THE BIBLE

The sacred text of Christianity is the Bible. The Bible is in two parts, the Old and the New Testaments. "Old" in this context means before Jesus Christ, and "New", after. The word "testament" means covenant. In other words, the Bible is divided in two parts because of two covenants: the first covenant was between God and the people of Israel (the Jews), and dominated by the name of Moses. The new covenant is the covenant of Jesus Christ, which Christians believe not only fulfils the expectations and hopes of the people of Israel, but also extends the blessings of the old covenant to the nations of the world, solely through Jesus' death and resurrection. The New Testament fulfils the hopes and dreams expressed in the Old Testament.

The Biblical Canon

The Old Testament comprises thirty-nine books, and the New Testament, twenty-seven; hence sixty-six in all. Together, these form the "canon", that is, the "measure" from which Christian life and belief is taken. The biblical canon is "closed", meaning nothing can be added to it or taken from it. There is another group of books called the Apocrypha (approximately fifteen books), dating from the period between the two Testaments (roughly 400 BC to 1 BC), which some Christians will use for personal edification. The Apocrypha is not canonical in that, on the whole, doctrine is not derived from it.

Key Ideas to Understand the Christian Bible

CANON

A canon is an authoritative collection of texts agreed either officially (by a council) or unofficially (widely accepted in a community). Different religious groupings have different canons. Christianity, in the main, accepts the Old and New Testaments as its canon. Other books and religious texts may be on the edges of canonicity.

A LIBRARY WITHIN A BOOK

The Bible contains different types of literature (including history, law, prophecy, gospel, poetry, songs, apocalyptic, journals, divine speech, sermons, proverbs, letters, visions, and genealogy) written over a period of 1,500 years (roughly 1400 BC to AD 100). The full sixty-six books hang together as a single story of God's relationship with his people. The Bible is self-verifying: in other words, later writers quote from earlier parts of the Bible, and it claims to have internal consistency, yet also development and commentary on itself. The Jewish canon was probably made during the Babylonian exile (sixth century BC); various Christian canons exist, but generally, the list of authoritative books was finalized by the fifth century AD.

THE OLD TESTAMENT

Genesis	Exodus	Leviticus	Numbers	Deuteronomy				Joshua	Judges	Ruth	1 Samuel	2 Samuel
1 Kings	2 Kings	1 Chronicles	2 Chronicles	Ezra	Nehemiah	Esther		Job	Psalms	Proverbs	Ecclesiastes	Song of Songs
Isaiah	Jeremiah	Lamentations	Ezekiel	Daniel	Hosea	Joel		Amos	Obadiah	Jonah	Micah	Nahum
Habakkuk	Zephaniah	Haggai	Zechariah	Malachi								

THE NEW TESTAMENT

					Matthew	Mark	Luke	John	Acts
Romans	1 Corinthians	2 Corinthians	Galatians	Ephesians	Philippians	Colossians	1 Thessalonians	2 Thessalonians	1 Timothy	2 Timothy	Titus
Philemon	Hebrews	James	1 Peter	2 Peter	1 John	2 John	3 John	Jude	Revelation		

KEY

PENTATEUCH	HISTORY	WISDOM WRITINGS	MAJOR PROPHETS	MINOR PROPHETS	GOSPEL NARRATIVES	ACTS NARRATIVES	PAUL'S LETTERS TO CHURCHES	PAUL'S LETTERS TO INDIVDUALS	GENERAL LETTERS	LETTER PROPHECY

SPECIFIC/SPECIAL REVELATION

The Bible claims that God chose to reveal himself to humanity. The Bible makes no argument for the existence of God; it merely assumes God exists. The opening verse reads "In the beginning God created the heavens and the earth" (Genesis 1:1). The Bible itself distinguishes between general and special revelation. General revelation is understood to be in creation and the conscience: everyone can know something about God. Special revelation is particular: the Bible is special revelation, and Jesus Christ himself is the full and final revelation of God. It follows that should one wish to know God, one can only do so through Jesus Christ, as revealed in the Bible.

INSPIRATION

Christians understand the Bible to be "inspired" – the sense that the Bible is "God-breathed" or "exhaled by God". Inspiration is not dictation (although some parts of the Bible are dictated divine speeches). It is a spiritual weaving between the "breathing out of God" and the will and personality of the writer – a unique combination of human writing in a way that is perfectly consistent with what God intended to be written. God guides the author in their writing, but does not override the author's style. Hence the Bible is a very human book – full of human joys and sorrows – and yet also a divine book, offering a storyline of God's relationship with the world, and God's plan of salvation to renew and transform all creation.

TRANSLATION

The Bible was written originally in the local languages: Hebrew, Aramaic, and Koine (common) Greek. It is not written in a "holy language". It is these original texts that are considered to be inspired, and yet none of the originals actually exist. The process of copying was so well organized, disciplined, and precise in ancient Israel that the texts we do have are generally regarded as being 99 per cent accurate. Because there are so many ancient fragments that do date back considerably close to the time to which they refer, cross-checking is easy. The Scriptures that Jesus had access to was the Septuagint, the standard Greek translation of the Hebrew Scriptures, translated into common Greek by seventy or seventy-two scholars in Alexandria (Egypt) in the third century BC. The Bible has a rich history of translation into the languages of the world. Full Bibles or Bible portions have been translated into 2,700 of the world's 6,900 living languages. In 2012, there were about 2,000 active Bible translation projects around the world.

DEAD SEA SCROLLS

The Dead Sea Scrolls were discovered by a shepherd boy in 1947 in caves near Qumran, Israel. Qumran was a monastic Essene community (a sect of Judaism characterized by its ascetic lifestyle), and the scrolls possibly formed part of their library. In total over 950 scrolls of biblical (and other) texts were found over a period of nine years. The collection contains the earliest known copies of the Hebrew Bible, as well as related manuscripts about Temple worship in Jerusalem. They date from between 400 and 300 BC and these texts – including major prophets like Isaiah – verified the accuracy of later copies of biblical texts, and also filled in many gaps in the history of the Jewish people, particularly in the period between the Old and New Testaments. Below is a sample of the so-called "Temple Scroll".

The ruins of the Essene community in Qumran.

Christianity

BELIEF AND PRACTICE

Like Judaism, Christianity is monotheistic – that is, Christians believe in one God. However, it is the belief in Jesus Christ as God that makes Christianity unique. In other words, God has visited this planet in person. The doctrine of the Trinity – the Father, Son, and Holy Spirit as one – lies at the heart of Christian belief. This is indeed a mystery, and many thinkers continue to struggle with this idea. Nevertheless, the Trinity can be thought of as a Tri-unity of equal relationship of love.

In practice, Christians strive to live a life devoted to God, as modelled by Jesus Christ and empowered by the Holy Spirit. They live with the hope that God's reign – which started explicitly in the coming of Jesus – will come to full expression when Jesus returns to usher in the final and complete reign of God in the new heavens and new earth.

CORE BELIEFS

ONE GOD

Christians believe there is only one God and that God is one. God is Spirit. God is creator and sustainer of the universe. God can be known through his Son, Jesus Christ, alone.

TRINITY

This idea is unique to Christianity. This one God is three persons: Father, Son, and Holy Spirit. Christianity does not have three separate gods. The use of the words "Father" and "Son" indicates the type of relationship, not the sexuality of God, or the subordination or dominance of either Father or Son.

Artists have grappled with trying to portray the Trinity in their work. In *The Holy Trinity,* Nicoletto (fl.1353–70) attempts to demonstrate the union, yet distnctiveness, of the Father and the Son, with the Spirit as a dove hovering between them.

INCARNATION

The Father sent the Son into the world as Jesus Christ. In other words, the Son "took on flesh" and became human (but without losing any deity). Christians celebrate this at Christmas time. After Jesus' ascension (his return to the Father), the Holy Spirit was given to Jesus' disciples as an ongoing living presence of God.

SIN

This word has a large range of meanings. It means a mistake, an intentional rebellion, "missing the mark", and moral corruption. God created humankind good and with free will, but humanity chose to rebel against God. This introduced sin into the universe (see Genesis 2–3).

HUMANITY

Humankind was made in the image of God, in that we have many of God's characteristics and qualities (for example, being relational, loving, creative, and imaginative). The Bible is clear, however, that humans are not gods, nor will they ever become God.

ATONEMENT

Humanity sinned – that is, rebelled against God – and hence God, because he is loving, wished to set things right. "Atonement" is an umbrella term describing at least five pictures that the apostle Paul uses in his New Testament writings to explain how God sets things right with humanity. These include: court of Law (justification); commerce (redemption); personal relationships (reconciliation); worship (sacrifice); battleground (victory over evil). This "setting things right" – atonement – was achieved through the death and resurrection of Jesus Christ.

RESURRECTION

On the Sunday after his crucifixion, Jesus was physically resurrected as a new type of living bodily existence, ushering in a new cosmic age. The Bible notes that Jesus is the "firstfruits" of resurrection, meaning his resurrection as the first will be followed in the future by the resurrection of everyone (see 1 Corinthians 15:20).

ETHICS

Love of God and love of neighbour motivates Christians for right living. It is not so much that God has made bad people good, but spiritually dead people alive. Hence this "life in its fullness" has propelled Christians into public service and the reformation of society. Many social movements have been started by Christians with this ethic: for example, the Salvation Army was formed in 1865 originally as a response to the dire social needs in Britain.

Christian Practices

Christians practise baptism (either sprinkling or full immersion in water) as an entry rite, and also Communion (Eucharist). Eucharist is a short drama in which bread, representing Christ's body, and wine, representing Christ's blood, are eaten and drunk by the participants. There are many variations of these two acts, with different understandings of what they actually achieve. Baptism usually happens only once in a lifetime, while Eucharist could be taken as often as daily.

Christians will also generally prioritize regular Bible reading, and seek to apply to life what they learn. Many practise tithing – giving 10 per cent of their income to their church or to special causes. Rhythms of prayer – daily, weekly, and yearly – are common. Most Christians meet on a Sunday for combined worship events in formal and informal gatherings, either in churches or in homes.

Christian Festivals

Different branches and denominations of Christian churches have various local festivals, but two are common to all.

- Christmas (25 December) is the time when Christians celebrate the incarnation of Jesus Christ, that is, God's coming to earth as the baby Jesus Christ, born in Bethlehem, Israel.

- Easter is the other major festival. This is lunar and shifts every year, but usually occurs in early April. It includes Good Friday and Easter Sunday, remembering the crucifixion of Jesus and the resurrection of Jesus, respectively.

Some denominations have a yearly cycle of festivals, either leading up to Christmas (Advent), or Easter (Lent), with subsequent special days as well. Epiphany (6 or 8 January) – the coming of the wise men to worship the new-born Jesus – is also widely celebrated. Some denominations will celebrate Pentecost (fifty days after Easter), recognizing when the Holy Spirit was gifted to the disciples in a dramatic way (Acts 2).

A young Orthodox Christian worshipper holds a large cross during a Good Friday procession on the Via Dolorosa, retracing the route Jesus Christ walked to his crucifixion in Jerusalem.

LORD'S PRAYER

Jesus' disciples once asked him "Lord, teach us to pray" (Luke 11:1–4). Responding to this simple request, Jesus taught them a prayer which many Christians recite by memory today, and which has become known as "The Lord's Prayer".

Our Father in heaven,
hallowed be your name,
your kingdom come,
your will be done,
on earth as in heaven.
Give us today our daily bread.
Forgive us our sins
as we forgive those who sin
against us.
Lead us not into temptation
but deliver us from evil.
For the kingdom, the power,
and the glory are yours
now and for ever.
Amen.

BEATITUDES

Jesus' so-called Sermon on the Mount (Matthew 5–7) is well loved by both Christians and people of other faiths. It starts with the well-known Beatitudes:

Blessed are the poor in spirit,
for theirs is the kingdom of heaven.

Blessed are those who mourn,
for they will be comforted.

Blessed are the meek,
for they will inherit the earth.

Blessed are those who hunger and thirst for righteousness,
for they will be filled.

Blessed are the merciful,
for they will be shown mercy.

Blessed are the pure in heart,
for they will see God.

Blessed are the peacemakers,
for they will be called children of God.

Blessed are those who are persecuted because of righteousness,
for theirs is the kingdom of heaven.

Matthew 5:1–10

Christianity

GOING GLOBAL

From its beginnings as a sect of Judaism, Christianity has spread rapidly and widely. This is consistent with the teaching of the Bible, right back to when Abraham and his descendants were called to be a "blessing to all the nations" (Genesis 12:2–3). The apostle Paul interprets the descendants of Abraham as people who have Abraham's faith, not his ethnic genealogy. Jesus himself told his disciples, "Therefore go and make disciples of all nations, baptizing them… and teaching them to obey everything I have commanded you" (Matthew 28:19–20).

The history of Christianity can be divided into several periods. Each represents the development of a distinct Christian belief or practice – a paradigm. Each of these paradigms represents certain "shifts" that have occurred in Christianity.

Primitive Christianity and the Eastern Church, AD 100–600

Christianity became the official religion of the Roman empire by the fourth century AD after years of persecution and wrangling over core beliefs. The life and love of God were emphasized; the call to community around liturgy was strong. Armenia was the first Christian nation in AD 301, and Christianity pushed along the Silk Road east to China.

Medieval and Roman Catholic Church, AD 600–1500

Christianity had been influenced by Augustine of Hippo (AD 354–430) who wrote *City of God* to interpret the fall of the Roman empire. According to Augustine, society was not only physical (the city of Rome), but also spiritual, and this spiritual city of God would never fall. Nevertheless, church and state were well on the way to being melded together: monks became "ideal citizens" and kings and popes kept Europe in a uniform religion – Christendom. This church/state union promoted the Crusades so as to expand this temporal "kingdom of God". The Crusades attempted to win back the Holy Land through warfare.

Portrait of Martin Luther (1483–1546) by Lucas Cranach the Elder.

Protestant Reformation, 1500–1800

The German monk Martin Luther sparked the Reformation in 1517, but reform had also been attempted before Luther. Getting right with God – justification – became a core idea, based on renewed reading of the Bible that was concurrently translated into the languages of Europe. With the invention of the printing press and moveable type, everyone could have access to the Bible. Core beliefs and practices of the Roman Catholic Church were challenged at the grassroots level. The catch cry became "by faith alone, by Scripture alone, by grace alone".

Enlightenment Christianity, 1800–2000

With the rise of human reason, science, and materialism, some of the core aspects of Christian faith were re-examined. Christianity both embraced this and reacted against it. Christianity got tangled up with colonial expansion. Asian, African, and Latin American churches eventually found their voices, yet this period is overshadowed with despotic governments and world wars. Persecution, "underground" Christianity, and the rise of Pentecostalism – emphasizing experience of the Holy Spirit – have all been aspects of this period.

Ecumenical, from 2000 to the Present

• •

Christianity continues to expand rapidly in the world, but in new ways. There is a shift from the Old World centres (Europe and America) to the newer "global south" centres, namely Africa, Asia, and Latin America. The church is growing fastest in these places. There is also a much richer conversation happening between Roman, Orthodox, and Protestant churches.

Christianity wrestles with culture, looking for appropriate united responses to the challenges of the twenty-first century. For example, women are gaining more influence in leadership, and issues related to sexuality are keenly debated. Many are thinking deeply about environmental concerns, and are politically proactive in standing for the poor in the face of corruption and exploitation by banking systems. Christians seek to find an appropriate balance between social justice initiatives and recognizing the call to preach the gospel – God's offer of salvation – to all. New and unique contextual theologies are emerging, such as Black theology, gay theology, liberation theology, and feminist theology. Christians are responding in new and innovative ways to the different world religions. They recognize that there must be open and honest conversation with people of other religions because globalism and migration bring people of others religions together. They ask, in what ways might God be at work in other religions, and how might Jesus Christ still be considered to be unique?

THE RISE OF PENTECOSTALISM

Christianity, like other religions, continues to experience various reform movements. In 1901 in California, the Pentecostal movement started when people experienced spiritual power in unprecedented ways. This movement emphasizes that Christians should be able to experience similar power as the first disciples did at Pentecost (Acts 2), including supernatural giftings of prophecy, healing, and speaking in tongues (a phenomenon in which one speaks in a new spiritual language). Pentecostalism has spread rapidly and is the fastest-growing part of the church in South America, Africa, and Asia.

ASIAN THEOLOGY

There is opportunity today for non-Western forms of Christianity to find their own voice. In Korea, *minjung* theology, or "theology of the people", has been a response to the industrialization of South Korea, its restrictive politics, and the marginalization of the worker. Appeals are made to Latin American "liberation theology" in which the poor have agitated for a more just place in decision making in the nation. In India, *Dalit* theology is a response by "out-castes" – those outside the Hindu caste system – who become Christians and model their hopes on Jesus Christ in that he too was an "outcast" in similar ways.

Islam

INTRODUCTION AND DEFINITIONS

From its beginnings in the seventh century AD in Arabia, Islam has grown to be a world religion with 1.6 billion members (22 per cent of the world's population). The main Muslim populations are found across North Africa, the Middle East, central and south Asia, and into South East Asia. Because of migration, there are Muslim populations in Europe (42 million) and America (2.6 million or 0.8 per cent of the population). Indonesia has the most Muslims of any country. In this vast spread, there are many different expressions of Islam. Islam is as varied as other religions with an equally rich tapestry of beliefs, rituals, and expressions.

In this rich variation there are elements that all Muslim communities have in common. The five pillars of Islam, the six beliefs, the Qur'an (in its Arabic text), the example of the prophet Muhammad, and the rhythm of festivals – these are familiar to all Muslims from Iceland to New Zealand.

SUBMISSION TO GOD

Islam is a complete way of life covering family, social, political, spiritual, religious, financial, community, and personal spheres. It is submission to God in all areas, public and private. The word *Din* is translated "religion" but is more fully the idea of a way of life, a complete and comprehensive path to follow. This can surprise people who are used to the idea of secularism (separation of religion and state) and who tend to see religion as private. There are Muslims who believe in secularism, and there are Muslim countries with secular constitutions, but the tendency is usually towards engagement of Islamic belief and practice with politics.

The Path of Islam

Islam teaches that the aim of life is to live a "successful" (*falah*) life, both now and in the next life. Success is the achievement of well-being and the protection from evil. Complete *falah* is understood to only be found in paradise, but is possible to some extent here and now. The call to prayer, which occurs five times a day, exhorts listeners to "come to success".

If well-being is the aim, then the problem is ignorance (*jahiliyyah*) and not knowing God's guidance. This stands in the way of people's success and well-being. And if this is the problem, then the solution is to know God's guidance (*huda*) and to submit to him. This guidance is provided in several ways: by the Qur'an, by the perfect example of Muhammad, in the writings of the *hadith* (statements and sayings of Muhammad), and by the outworkings of *sharia* (law and moral code).

A Way of Life

The Islamic way covers all areas of life. From what one eats (*halal* and *haram*), to the way one dresses, to greetings and farewells, to the daily rhythm of life, to the yearly cycles and the wholeness of one's outlook, the way of Islam sets out the path on which one walks. Life's activities vary from being forbidden (*haram*) to obligatory (*Wajib*), with many being neutral. This helps provide the road markers along the way. This path is modelled on the prophet Muhammad and the teaching of the Qur'an. It follows then that it is important for Muslims to know the history and story of the prophet.

S-L-M (س ل م)

This Arabic root carries the sense of wholeness or completeness and therefore it is the foundation for peace (*salaam*) in that one is complete/whole. (It is also related to the Hebrew word *shalom*.)

- **Islam** – complete submission (to God), that is, entrusting one's wholeness to God.

- **Muslim** – one who submits to God.

- **Salaam** – peace and wholeness (through submitting to God).

Left: Hagia Sophia, the Church of the Holy Wisdom, was formerly a Byzantine church, then an Ottoman mosque, and is now a museum in Istanbul, Turkey. Commissioned by Emperor Justinian I, it is a fine example of Byzantine architecture. The interior decoration shows Islamic elements throughout.

● SEE ALSO
BAHAI PP. 106–107

WHO IS A MUSLIM?

The phrase "the Muslim world" is an unhelpful generalization, for among its many groups it includes:

- Bengali-speaking Muslims with a philosophy very similar to Tantric Buddhism

- Farsi-speaking Muslims deeply influenced by Greek philosophy

- Arabic-speaking Salafi-style Muslims who are strict and pious in their practice

- tribal African Muslims deeply influenced by an animistic outlook

The term "Muslim" covers theological, linguistic, cultural, political, and economic differences. This breadth can sometimes be overlooked.

VOCAB FOR EVERYDAY PRACTICE OF ISLAM

Strict regulations govern everyday actions, which vary from being obligatory to prohibited.

- *Wajib* (or *fard*): obligatory, e.g. performing daily prayers (*salat*), giving alms (*zakat*)

- *Mustahabb/Sunnah*: recommended, e.g. reciting the Qur'an, or visiting the sock or other voluntary charity (*Sadaqah*)

- *Mubah*: neutral (neither obligatory nor recommended), e.g. reading, eating, playing sport

- *Makruh*: abominable (abstaining is recommended), e.g. taking bribes and eating some food, such as prawns

- *Haram*: prohibited (abstaining is obligatory), e.g. idolatry, murder, various food (such as pork), and alcohol

THE "STRAIGHT WAY"

The phrase "Show us the straight way" is said twice in each of the five daily prayer times. It is part of a longer section from the Qur'an:

Show us the straight way,
The way of those on whom
Thou has bestowed Thy Grace,
Those whose (portion)
Is not wrath,
And who go not astray.

Sura 1.6, 7

Islam

MUHAMMAD

Muslims believe that the prophet Muhammad was a messenger of God, the last prophet sent by God ("the Seal of the Prophets"). Disagreement over the question of who would succeed Muhammad after his death as leader of the Muslim community led to the establishment of two distinct groups, the Sunni and Shi'a. An overview of Muhammad's life is important for understanding how Islam was born.

Location of the Islamic holy cities of Mecca and Medina.

Muhammad's Early Life

Born in AD 570 in Mecca (in today's Saudi Arabia), Muhammad was orphaned by the age of six. As was the fashion of the tribal system of Arabia, he was then brought up by his uncle, Abu Talib, and joined Abu Talib in his merchant business. As a merchant Muhammad earned himself the nickname "Al Amin" ("The trustworthy"). At the age of twenty-five he married a rich widow (Khadija), the owner of a merchant business of her own, which he then managed. Muhammad was thus a well-travelled man, well respected, and he had some experience of other cultures and religions.

The *Kaaba* is a cuboid building in the centre of the Masjid-al-Haram mosque in Mecca, Saudi Arabia. It is significant for Muslims in many ways and is associated variously with Abraham, Ishmael, angels, Muhammad, and the Qur'an. For Muslims it represents one of the oldest places of worship of Allah. The *Kaaba* is the focal point of prayer, as well as pilgrimage, particularly the annual *hajj*.

Muhammad's Revelation

Muhammad grew into the habit of taking time out and going to the caves in the hills around Mecca to meditate and pray. When he was forty years old, he had a profound spiritual experience. He had a vision of the angel Gabriel, who told him to recite (or read) words revealed to him. This was an overwhelming experience. Through the support of his wife and through further experiences he came to see himself as a prophet, a messenger of warning from the one God to people who did not know him and who were engaged in idolatry. The message, at its simplest, was "There is no God but God" and Muhammad is his messenger.

At the time, Mecca had a religious sanctuary known as the *Kaaba* that housed many images. This was a site of pilgrimage for devotees – probably the nomadic Bedouin – before Islam gained traction. It was therefore a source of income for the Meccans. So, in a city devoted to the reverence and worship of images, and reliant on the economic benefits from those on pilgrimage, Muhammad's monotheism was not a welcome message. Nevertheless, a small group of followers emerged who cherished these ongoing revelations.

However, following the deaths of his wife Khadija and uncle Abu Talib, and with the loss of two of his greatest supporters, persecution against Muhammad grew. A solution to this predicament was needed.

A Narrow Escape

In the town of Yathrib there were four clans, each vying for power. Muhammad was known to some of them, and they approached him to ask whether he would come to be the leader of the town. This seemed to be a poisoned chalice as, in all likelihood, each group would have been vying to gain control of him. However, the offer included safety, and so over a period of a few weeks, Muhammad's followers quietly left for Yathrib, until it was just Muhammad and his son-in-law, Ali. A group of Meccan men had planned to assassinate Muhammad, and on the chosen night they broke into his rooms to find Ali had taken his place. Muhammad had fled. Amazed at this devotion they followed his tracks to a cave in the hills. At the entrance of the cave they found a nesting pigeon and a spider's web covering the entrance. Reasoning that he couldn't be in there, they headed north to search for him, again missing the chance to kill him.

Muhammad's Growing Influence

In AD 622, Muhammad entered the town of Yathrib to take up leadership there. The first decision he needed to make was to find a neutral place to stay without looking to favour any of the four clans. He set his camel loose and declared that where it stopped, there he would reside. This diplomatic strategy was a mark of his emerging leadership. To feed and support his followers who had come from Mecca, Muhammad needed an income. So he took to raiding merchants' camel trains. This had the effect of bringing an income into Yathrib (now called Medina – the city of the prophet), placing Muhammad in the position of signing treaties with other tribes and their merchants, and continuing to challenge the Meccans economically. This led to a series of three battles with the Meccans. The Muhammadans won the first, lost the second (but were left intact), and in the third they built a trench defence that meant the Meccans were powerless to attack. In this more and more groups joined the increasingly powerful followers of Muhammad.

Return to Mecca

Muhammad eventually was able to lead his followers on a pilgrimage to Mecca, under the protection offered to all pilgrims; however, they were denied entry. At Mecca there were negotiations wherein Muhammad agreed to return the following year, at which time the Meccans would allow them entry. Although some in the Muhammadan group felt that they were backing down, Muhammad saw the wisdom in it. The following year, they did return, at which time the Meccans let them in and became Muslim themselves. The images in the *Kaaba* were destroyed but the practice of pilgrimage was to continue. The *Kaaba* remains the focal point of Muslim devotion, and has become associated with the story of Abraham. Muslims all over the world pray in the direction of the *Kaaba*. It is also the destination of pilgrims every year at the *hajj* festival.

THE HIJRA

The *Hijra* is the move from Mecca to Yathrib (now Medina) that occurred in AD 622. This became year zero of the Islamic calendar. This is seen as more significant than Muhammad's birth or his first revelation. It is the foundation of Muhammad in the role of prophet–statesman and the birth of Islam as a theo-political entity.

WAS MUHAMMAD "ILLITERATE"?

Most Muslims believe Muhammad was illiterate. The reference means "unlettered" and may mean that he was unschooled though he may have learned some reading and writing skills as a merchant. The Arabic style and poetry of the Qur'an are exceedingly skilled and it is seen as a miracle that this could come through an unlettered man.

Islam

THE HOLY SCRIPTURES

The Qur'an is the holy book of Islam. It is arranged in 114 *suras* (chapters), and each *sura* is divided into *ayats* (verses). The Qur'an is understood to be the collection of the revelations given by God (Allah) to Muhammad. This is seen as a gradual revealing of a heavenly copy of the Qur'an. It is spoken of as being "sent down" (*tanzil*). Muhammad was therefore a means through which the Qur'an was revealed, but, as it is dictation, he did not shape it in any way. Nevertheless, Muhammad is viewed as embodying all that the Qur'an calls for, and Muslims idealize him as someone who lived out the Qur'an's teaching perfectly.

The revelations are in Arabic poetry and initially were memorized by Muhammad's followers. However, in one battle in which seventy of those who had memorized the Qur'an were killed, it became clear that the text needed to be written down. Over time slightly different versions of this written Qur'an began to develop. The fourth Muslim leader (*caliph*) was so concerned by this that he ordered all written versions to be brought together and six standard versions sent to cities in the growing Islamic sphere of influence. It can be said then that the Qur'an has been kept through oral transmission followed by textual tradition.

The Importance of Recitation

The Qur'an is viewed as only being authentic when in the Arabic language. Versions in other languages are not seen as translations but as interpretations or paraphrases. About 80 per cent of Muslims around the world do not speak Arabic. Yet many Muslims learn how to recite it word perfect in Arabic. The verbal recitation of the Qur'an is seen as speaking and hearing the words of heaven itself, with all the grace and power that this brings by being in touch with the divine.

SURA

In the Qur'an, the *sura* are organized from longest to shortest, which means they are not arranged chronologically or thematically. The words themselves are considered to be eternal, and hence the historical sequence and themes are less important. Reading the Qur'an therefore requires a separate knowledge of the context. This information comes from the biographies of Muhammad and the collections of sayings, the *hadith*.

The *Hadith*

When Muhammad was alive he was able to explain the meaning of the revelations. After he died (AD 632) both the chronology of his life, and the context of the Qur'an's chapters began to be understood and interpreted in new ways. Islam was also spreading, with new leaders who had not known Muhammad coming into power in new lands; hence a number of stories evolved. Some were true, some were made up to suit political means, and some stories were additions made from memory. Together they form the *hadith*.

These *hadith* were gathered and assessed by different writers three centuries after the death of Muhammad. This was an immense task of deciding the authenticity of thousands of sayings. The measure used for deciding whether a saying was authentic was the reported chain of transmission (*isnad*), focusing on the reliability of the people named in the transmission. Nevertheless, Sunni and Shi'a denominations of Islam have different *hadith*.

An individual *hadith* will have text and narrators (*isnad*). Each one reports an action of Muhammad, or his criticism or approval of different issues. The content is used for guidance in the everyday Muslim way of life.

SCHOLARLY STUDY OF THE QUR'AN AND HADITH

Today some are beginning to ask questions of the standard story of the revelation of the Qur'an. Very early copies of the Qur'an are rare, and in those that have been found there are slight textual variations. These findings are contentious, because of the belief that God (Allah) had directly communicated to Muhammad.

The *hadith* were collected several hundred years after Muhammad's death. Relying on a chain of transmitters as the means of verification has led some to be suspicious of the truth-value of the *hadith*. Most Muslim scholars do not deny that there are false *hadith*, but claim that scholars have eliminated these.

Some Muslim groups claim that the Qur'an alone should be the source of guidance, and they reject the use of *hadith*. This is not a common response and most see *hadith* as essential for faith.

THE QUR'AN: AN EXCERPT (SURA 2.255)

God! There is no god
But He, – the Living,
The Self-subsisting, Eternal.
No slumber can seize Him
Nor sleep. His are all things
In the heavens and on earth.
Who is there can intercede
In His presence except
As He permitteth? He knoweth
What (appeareth to His creatures
As) Before and After
Or Behind them.
Nor shall they compass
Aught of His knowledge
Except as He willeth.
His Throne doth extend Over the heavens
And the earth, and He feeleth
No fatigue in guarding
And preserving them
For He is the Most High,
The Supreme (in Glory).

A portion of the Qur'an in the Maghrib script (North Africa), dating from the 13th century.

Islam

BELIEFS AND PRACTICES

"Islam" means "submission", and Muslims regard therefore that all of life – all the beliefs and practices of Islam – should demonstrate one's submission to Allah. Islam gives its followers a rhythm to life to work out this submission to Allah.

Islam has "five pillars", where belief and practice are so integrated that life and worship are "supported" by them. Considered obligatory by believers, these acts are the foundation of Muslim life.

Muslims bow during midday Friday prayers at a mosque in Kuwait City, Kuwait.

The Five Pillars of Islam

1. *Shahada* – the declaration of witness. This central confessional creed is "I testify that there is no God but God (Allah) and Muhammad is the prophet of God." It is said at times of prayer, it is the first thing whispered into a newborn baby's ear, it is said as someone dies, and saying it with intent is the act of converting to Islam.

2. *Salat* – prayers. The community prayers give a routine to life from morning to evening. Before prayers there is ritual washing to symbolize purification. Prayers are normally said at a mosque but, if using a prayer mat, can be said wherever one may be at the time of the call to prayer. The person praying faces the city of Mecca in Saudi Arabia (where the *Kaaba* is, the most sacred site in Islam), and mosques have a direction marker called a *qibla* for this purpose.

3. *Zakat* – almsgiving. This is 2.5 per cent of one's capital. In practice this is usually worked out with respect to how much cash is in pocket, rather than the value of gross capital. The reason for *zakat* is twofold: to help the poor, and to purify the giver from the lure of money. Money as *zakat* may also be given to help in mission and to win converts.

4. *Sawm* – fasting. The month of *Ramadan* is the month of fasting: people abstain from eating, drinking, and sex during sunlight hours. The day's fast is broken by a communal meal (*iftar*) at sunset. Those who are sick, pregnant, or travelling are exempt, but are required to make the time up. The festival of *Eid al Fitr* (Festival of Fast-breaking) is at the end of the month.

5. *Hajj* – the pilgrimage to Mecca. All those who are able are expected to make this pilgrimage at least once in their life. It is a time of self-purification and joining with millions of others in actions that focus on prayer around the *Kaaba* in Mecca. *Eid al Adha* (Festival of Sacrifice) comes at the end of this time, remembering Abraham's willingness to sacrifice his son.

Jihad

Some also consider *jihad* ("struggle") to be a pillar of Islam. The Qur'an speaks of *jihad* over forty times. Someone who "struggles" – that is, engages in *jihad* – is called *mujahedeen*. Most understand the term to be spiritual. Some argue that Islam promotes violence. Broadly, *jihad* covers a believer's internal struggle to live out the Muslim faith successfully, to build a Muslim society, and to defend Islam militarily if necessary. This latter idea reflects Muhammad's historical context, but *jihad* has come to be seen as any "holy war" by some.

The Calendar and Festivals

The Islamic calendar has twelve lunar months so the year is eleven days shorter than the Gregorian/Christian solar year. Five daily prayers, Friday prayers, and various festivals dictate the rhythm of the year.

- The Muslim New Year is the remembrance of the *Hijra* when Muhammad fled to Medina in AD 622.

- The Shi'a festival of Muharram is in the first month. It recalls the death of Muhammad's grandson (Hussain).

- In the third month is a remembrance of the birthdate of Muhammad (Milad un Nabi).

- In the seventh month is remembrance of Muhammad's night journey to heaven

- The eighth month includes all-night prayer vigils, because the Night of Power is when Allah determines the destiny of all people in the coming year.

- Ramadan is the ninth month of fasting. Ramadan ends with the large festival of Eid al Fitr, and is a communal time of feasting, almsgiving, and celebration.

- The Hajj is in the last month and concludes with the sacrifice Eid al Adha.

The Six Articles of Faith

Muslims embrace six key ideas that are foundational to their faith.

1. THE ONENESS OF ALLAH (GOD)

The *Shahada* declares there is no God but God, and the greatest sin (shirk) is associating anything with Allah. Islam therefore does not tolerate images of Allah.

2. THE DOCTRINE OF ANGELS

Islam teaches the existence of angels – spiritual beings who help people and record their actions. This also implies other spirit beings, known as *jinn* (hence the Arabian stories of genies – *jinn*). Indeed many Muslims see their life immersed in a world of spirit beings, some of whom are dangerous and unclean.

3. THE DOCTRINE OF APOSTLES

Muhammad is seen as the last and final *rasul* (apostle or messenger). Hence Adam, Musa (Moses), Nuh (Noah), Ibrihim (Abraham), and Isa (Jesus) are honoured in the Qur'an, but are not given the priority of Muhammad.

4. THE DOCTRINE OF THE BOOKS (REVELATIONS)

Islam recognizes that other prophets brought other scriptures (Moses brought the Tawrat or Torah, King David the Zabur or Psalms, and Jesus the Injil or Gospel) but these have become corrupted. The Qur'an is seen as the culmination and seal of the others: it is the literal word of God and the greatest piece of Arabic literature.

5. THE DOCTRINE OF LAST JUDGMENT AND LIFE AFTER DEATH

Muhammad's message was a call to turn from idolatry because there is a judgment coming of heaven and hell. The Qur'an teaches that, at the resurrection, no one can be sure of salvation, but people's deeds are recorded and at the end will be weighed on scales.

6. THE DOCTRINE OF PREDESTINATION

Allah is seen as all powerful and therefore preordains all that happens. Therefore the idea of God's will (Insh'allah) – God's governance and guidance – is core in a Muslim's approach to life.

Festivals of Islam

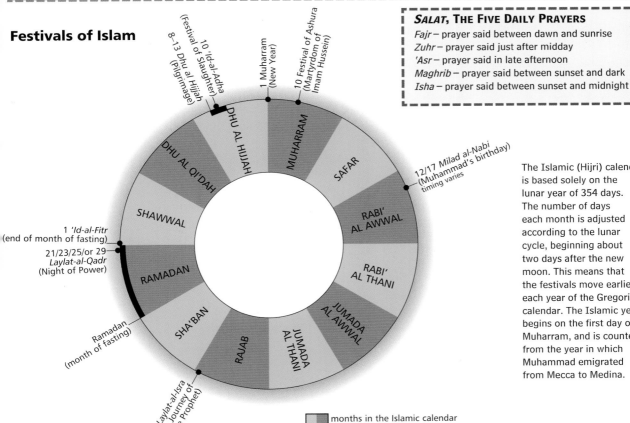

SALAT, THE FIVE DAILY PRAYERS

Fajr – prayer said between dawn and sunrise
Zuhr – prayer said just after midday
'Asr – prayer said in late afternoon
Maghrib – prayer said between sunset and dark
Isha – prayer said between sunset and midnight

10 'Id-al-Adha (festival of Slaughter)
8–13 Dhu al Hijjah (Pilgrimage)

1 Muharram (New Year)

10 Festival of Ashura (Martyrdom of Imam Hussein)

DHU AL HIJJAH
DHU AL QI'DAH
SHAWWAL
RAMADAN
SHA'BAN
RAJAB
JUMADA AL THANI
JUMADA AL AWWAL
RABI' AL THANI
RABI' AL AWWAL
SAFAR
MUHARRAM

12/17 Milad al-Nabi (Muhammad's birthday) timing varies

1 'Id-al-Fitr (end of month of fasting)

21/23/25/or 29 Laylat-al-Qadr (Night of Power)

Ramadan (month of fasting)

27 Laylat-al-Isra (Night Journey of the Prophet)

months in the Islamic calendar

The Islamic (Hijri) calendar is based solely on the lunar year of 354 days. The number of days each month is adjusted according to the lunar cycle, beginning about two days after the new moon. This means that the festivals move earlier each year of the Gregorian calendar. The Islamic year begins on the first day of Muharram, and is counted from the year in which Muhammad emigrated from Mecca to Medina.

Islam

SUNNI, SHI'A, AND SUFI

There are two major forms of Islam, known as Sunni (approximately 85 per cent of the world's Muslim population) and Shi'a (approximately 15 per cent of the world's Muslim population). Shi'a Muslims are mainly based in Iran but extend across into Iraq and other Middle Eastern countries to the west, and into Pakistan and south Asia in the east. The difference between Sunni and Shi'a centres around who should have led the new movement after the prophet Muhammad's death. The Sunni say it should have been leadership by deserving, able leaders, and the Shi'a believe it should have been by relatives of the prophet Muhammad. This tension came to a head with the death of Muhammad's grandson Hussein Ibn Ali (AD 626–680), which Shi'a see as a betrayal and an assassination by the Sunni. This event is remembered at the festival of *Muharram* (around the tenth day of the first month on the Islamic lunar calendar): the festival emphasizes the idea of sacrifice, sometimes demonstrated by self-flagellation (whipping oneself).

Sema, or *sama*, dancing is known to Europeans as the dance of the Whirling Dervishes or as Sufi whirling.

Sufism

Over time many Muslims became focused on mysticism: this became known as Sufism. Sufi spiritual guides (*Pirs* or *Shayekhs*) teach a path to spiritual union with the divine. Asceticism is common, as is meditation on the names of God. Although spread right across the countries where Islam is dominant,

Map showing the areas of influence of Sunnis and Shias.

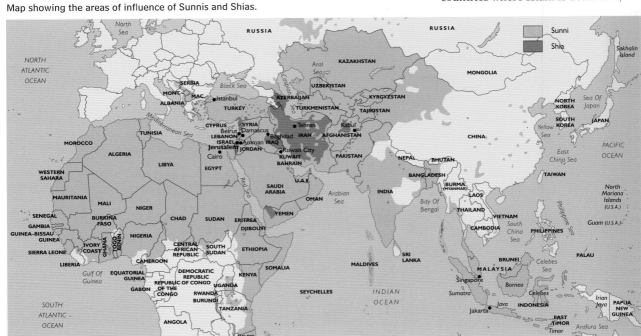

Islam has become a truly global religion due to migration flow and intentional expansion. It is now common to see the minarets of mosques in any major city of the world. This is just one example: the Islamic cultural Center, Manhattan, New York, USA.

ISLAMIC FUNDAMENTALISM

Religious fundamentalism is not unique to Islam. Fundamentalism as an ideology is also found in Christianity, Hinduism, Sikhism, Buddhism, secularism, and elsewhere. Fundamentalism is a term coined in the early 1900s in a Christian context in California. Fundamentalism is one of the responses to the perceived spiritual dryness of modernism, and the marginalization of the sacred. There is a return to the "fundamentals", that is, the perceived pure, or core, beliefs and rituals of a religion, in the face of perceived persecution, and the perception of being pushed to the margins.

Islamic fundamentalism has taken form – as interpreted by Western commentators – in the Wahhabi movement in Saudi Arabia, the 1979 Iranian revolution, the Taliban in Afghanistan, and the move to *sharia* law in some countries. The influence and actions of Al Qaeda worldwide, and the social constraints placed on women, are also informed by fundamentalist interpretations of Islam.

Despite the political rhetoric in the West, particularly since 9/11, most Muslims are people who just want to live a life that is successful and peaceful, relating to their families and neighbours. Like adherents of other religions, their lives and faith are shaped by their interactions in the varied contexts in which they find themselves.

Sufism is particularly influential in north Africa, Turkey, Iraq and south Asia, where the veneration of saints' graves and yoga-like practices have earned the ire of many Islamic purists.

Spirits

With the belief in angels, many Muslims also see themselves living in a world surrounded by evil spirits, *jinn*, and spirit powers. The evil eye, cursing, healing, fertility, and prosperity can therefore be interpreted using language drawn from magic. This is sometimes termed "folk Islam", but this gives the misleading impression that it is one uniform movement with shared practices. There are many forms of folk Islam, and these too are frowned upon by purists within Islam.

Salafi

Islamic purists are sometimes called *Salafi* ("those who look to the predecessors") or fundamentalists, a word that refers to those who look to the basic principles of the faith (though this is not a term liked by many Muslims). There are many types of Islamic purism, that is, movements seeking the "pure" essence of Islam. These include theological purist movements (for example, Deobandi and Tablighi Jamaat in India), political movements (Wahhabism in Saudi Arabia and Jamaat-i-Islami in south Asia), and violent *jihad*-motivated groups. When hearing about a group that is described as fundamentalist, it is important to clarify what combination of these three elements are included in their outlook.

Streams of Islam

Islam can be broadly talked of as having different streams. Two of these, Sunni and Shi'a, are formalized historically and doctrinally, and could be considered "denominations". Within these two groupings are Sufi and "folk" expressions of Islam.

Yoruba Religion and Voodoo

FROM AFRICA TO THE WORLD

The Yoruba are a broad collection of people in south-west Nigeria, Benin, Togo, and Sierra Leone, whose religion – Ifa – has influenced particularly the Caribbean, Brazil, and Colombia.

The Ifa religion of the Yoruba – or simply "Yoruba religion" – is today a blend of African divination religion and the

Roman Catholicism that the Yoruba encountered when they came to the Caribbean. Sometimes the religion is called Afro-Catholic folk religion. This mix of African and Catholic traditions has given rise to Voodoo. Initially Yoruba religion went with African slaves to the Americas in the seventeenth century, but has mainstreamed and now gone global due to migration and media: Caribbean immigrants to the United States and United Kingdom after the Second World War, for example, brought their Yoruba religion with them. The themes of Voodoo and zombie-ism in Western films are sourced partly from Yoruba ideas.

In Africa alone, the Yoruba number around 19 million. Adding in the Caribbean and South American countries pushes the numbers of adherents to around 100 million. The Caribbean island nations of Haiti, Puerto Rico, and the Dominican Republic are perhaps the best-known examples of explicit Yoruba/Voodoo.

Core Beliefs and Practices

In some sense, and like other tribal or "primal" religions, Yoruba is more about doing things, rather than believing: it is a pragmatic way of living. Telling a good story and delivering a good performance outweighs any systematic expression of belief or doctrine. Yoruba is dominated by divination: getting the divination rituals right is important so one lives well with the spirits.

Yoruba/Voodoo emphasizes humans' relationships between the living and the dead, including the ancestors, and also the unseen deities and spirits. Along with divination, spirit possession, animal sacrifice, music, and dance are highly valued. Yoruba believe that humans have more than one soul (usually at least two), and they affirm reincarnation: hence it is possible to lose one's soul (or have it stolen), or to function on less than the optimum number of souls (and fall sick because of it). Natural cycles of life and death are therefore important: zombies are those people who have had their souls stolen by spirits and/or sorcery.

Voodoo master Baron Samedi, a character in the *Live and Let Die* (1973) Bond film.

The High God Olodumare

Nevertheless, there is a positive side to Yoruba/Voodoo. Care of the soul through divination ensures a healthy body: hence the cure from physical sickness is associated with the removal of evil spirits. Additionally, believers can choose where their soul is to be reborn by submitting their request to the High God Olodumare (also called Olorun). Olodumare then allows them to choose their own destinies, and their own unique portions of good and bad luck.

However, the problems of humanity, as the Yoruba see it, are forgetfulness and disconnectedness. People forget the good things that Olodumare has given them and become disconnected from Olodumare. The cure is remembering. When they remember, they can then live up to the destiny for which Olodumare made them.

Orishas

The Yoruba universe is populated by deities called *Orishas* – more than 400 of them – who help people remember their destinies. *Orishas* are spirits of nature (for example, river, ocean, thunder) and also deified ancestors. The boundary of humanity and *Orishas* is not defined: hence the supernatural world and the material world are one. Priests then are needed (*babalawos* and *iyalawos*) to mediate. *Ashe* is sought: power to make things happen and fulfil one's destiny. The goal is to thrive now, here in this life, to find the balance and connection between human and *Orisha*.

Yoruba/Voodoo is syncretistic (that is, a fusion of different religious traditions) and reshapes and adapts to the culture that hosts it. *Orisha* shrines in Africa, for example, changed to houses in the Caribbean. Because Voodoo is so intertwined in everyday life in Haiti, François Duvalier, former President of Haiti (1957–71), manipulated people's belief in Voodoo to win political support. Voodoo now finds open expression among immigrant communities in many of the world's big cities: New York, London, Miami, Los Angeles, and Toronto are examples. Yoruba has also found expression among white Americans and the wider Latin American cultures. Its growing influence places it among the top ten global religions. The Catholic and the Voodoo characteristics are continually revised and modified.

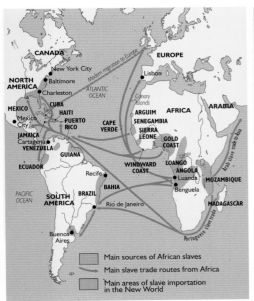

A Haitian voodoo ceremony.

TRANSPORT TO THE CARIBBEAN: NEW WORLD TRANSFORMATIONS

When the Yoruba arrived in the French colony of Haiti as slaves in the seventeenth century, Catholicism was the main religion. Yoruba had met Catholicism before in Africa: it was the religion of the Portuguese colonizers from the fifteenth century. This more generic "African folk religion" sustained the lives of the slaves. The slaves reinvented the *Orishas* as Catholic saints: Ogun is St Peter; Yejoma is Our Lady of Regla; Oya is St Theresa. This is also partly because slaves were dislocated from their ancestors in Africa, and hence ancestral *Orishas* were forgotten.

Jainism

A PEACEFUL RELIGION

Jainism is a small but significant religion. There are perhaps 6 million Jains worldwide, with 4 million adherents in India, its country of origin. For example, there are approximately 25,000 immigrant Jains in the United Kingdom, and there are small but recognizable groups in the United States: Houston, for example, has a population of about 600 active Jains.

Jainism is one of India's oldest religions. It grew simultaneously with Hinduism, and was also influenced by Buddhism. As in Hinduism and Buddhism, the concepts of *karma*, reincarnation, ethics, and asceticism are also part of Jain belief.

At the Temple of Adinath in Ranakpur, India, a Jain pilgrim prepares to make a ritual offering, or *puja*, of wild roses, sandalwood paste, saffron, and camphor to the saints. He covers his nose and mouth so as not to inadvertently swallow any insects or smell the fragrant scents of his offerings.

Jainism's Founder

Mahavira (c. 599–527 BC) is generally credited as the leader of Jainism. He didn't found Jainism as much as restore, reform, and popularize practices, beliefs, and a way of life that were common – yet often dormant – in the Indian collective worldview.

Mahavira was born a prince of the *Kshatriya* (warrior) caste, in a village in what is now Bihar state, India. He left the palace at age thirty, soon after his parents had died, to live the life of an ascetic. "Mahavira" is a title; he was born Prince Vardhamana. On becoming an ascetic, Vardhamana undertook severe fasting and meditation, managing to attain *kevalnyan* (enlightenment), and hence the title "Mahavira", meaning "great hero".

Beliefs and Practices

AHIMSA

Jainism's central virtue is *ahimsa* – non-violence or, more specifically, non-injury to all living things. This is because all living things have soul, and should therefore be treated with equal value: if one kills a soul, then there are bad consequences for one's *karma*.

Jains are strict vegetarians, but they can also be readily recognized in public because of their concern not to crush or imbibe anything living. Monks will be seen sweeping the path in front of them, in order to avoid treading on any living thing and killing it. They sometimes wear masks and strain their drinking water so as not to swallow any insects.

> While *ahimsa* is the highest ideal, there are also three guiding principles to life:
> 1. Right belief
> 2. Right knowledge
> 3. Right conduct

TAPAS

As well as requiring mental training, Jainism emphasizes physical austerities, or *tapas*. These are widely practised in India generally, but heightened to their extreme in Jainism. For example, the noblest ideal in Jainism is for a saint to starve himself to death.

ABSENCE OF A DEITY OR CREATOR

There are no deities in Jainism, or, more precisely, Jains are agnostic (they believe it is impossible to know whether God or gods exist). There is no creator. They believe that the universe is in the shape of a giant human, and humans in this current world age are located about its waist. A soul with good *karma* will rise to the top of the cosmic man, free from pain and movement. All souls are omniscient – all-knowing – and yet are defiled by loss of knowledge. Jainism is essentially a religion of self-help. Liberation is the return to omniscience through correct knowledge, gained through ascetic disciplines.

Jain Sects

There are two main sects of Jainism: the *Digambara* ("sky-clad") and the *Svetambara* ("white-clad"). This refers to how they are dressed: the "sky-clad" ideally wear nothing, as evidence of extreme asceticism, while the "white-clad" wear simple white garments.

Jain Scriptures

The teachings of Mahavira are called the *Agamas*. These are based on memorized words: because monks and nuns were not allowed to acquire possessions, they could not write his words down in books. As commentaries on these sayings grew, the volume of words that had to be memorized grew as well. Over time the corpus has become compromised due to loss of memory (and the fact that it was largely unwritten). Severe famine in 350 BC killed many monks, and the memorized tradition was broken.

The *Agamas* are canonical for the *Svetambara* sect: they believe an adequate number of *sutras* survived the famine. The *Digambara* believe all the *Agamas* were lost. Because of this, the role scriptures play in the two sects is different. Monks and nuns are now permitted to own religious texts.

The texts are not valued necessarily because Mahavira said them, but because they represent eternal, endless, yet fixed truths: they are believed to represent a tradition without divine or human origin.

THE FORDMAKERS

Mahavira is thought to be the last of twenty-four *trithankaras* or "fordmakers". A fordmaker is someone who shows others how to "cross over" – like fording a river – to the other shore of existence. Jain temples contain images of the "fordmakers".

INFLUENCE IN INDIA

Because Jains could not be agricultural workers for fear of harming living things (ploughing, for example, kills worms), Jains have tended to be merchants and artisans. Because of this, those who have not taken vows of asceticism have found themselves often with quite some influence in the economy of India.

Sculpture of Mahavira at the Jain Temple in Jaisalmer, Rajasthan, India. Within the Jaisalmer Fort is a complex of seven yellow sandstone Jain temples dating from the 12th to 16th century.

> ### THE FIVE *MAHAVRATAS* (ASCETIC VOWS)
>
> The *mahavratas* are taken as part of a Jain's spiritual journey to *moksha* (liberation of the soul).
> 1. A commitment to non-violence
> 2. Non-attachment to possessions
> 3. Not lying
> 4. Not stealing
> 5. Sexual restraint (celibacy is the ideal)

Zoroastrianism

AND THE PARSEES OF MUMBAI

Originating in the eastern part of modern Iran, Zoroastrianism is one of the world's most ancient monotheistic religions – it originally honoured only one god, Ahura Mazda. Possibly 2,900 years old, it was founded by the prophet Zoroaster. There is some disagreement as to when he lived: estimates range from between the seventh and the tenth centuries BC. The name Zoroaster is a Greek form of the word "Zarathustra".

Zoroaster protested against religious features of his day: he resisted the warrior culture, the sacrifice of bulls, and the use of hallucinogenic drugs for spiritual ecstasy. Hence he subverted the establishment to some degree.

However, in its heyday, Zoroastrianism became one of the most influential religions in the world: it was the official religion of Persia for a thousand years (c. 600 BC–AD 650). Today, it is possibly one of the smallest religions in the world, with adherents as few as 190,000 worldwide. However, a modern derivative of Zoroastrianism, the Parsees (Parsis), are influential in the western Indian city of Mumbai (Bombay): here they number only 70,000 or so, but have a huge influence in business and industry.

Beliefs

Ahura Mazda – the "Wise Lord" – is the one God of Zoroastrianism. He fathered twin spirits Spenta Mainyu (Benevolent Spirit) and Angra Mainyu (Hostile Spirit): originally these two spirits made a choice: one for good, the other for evil. Hence now each person likewise makes a similar choice, for good or evil. Zoroastrianism is therefore dualistic: good and evil, light and dark, oppose each other. There is both cosmic dualism and moral dualism: two equal powers struggle in the universe and two equal powers – good and evil – struggle in the minds of people.

THE SCRIPTURES

The Zoroastrian holy book is the Avesta, compiled around the sixth century AD but made up of materials hundreds of years older. There are two sections: the older part contains the *gathas* – seventeen hymns thought to have been composed by Zoroaster himself. The newer or younger part of the Avesta is a commentary on the older part, and also contains some myths, stories, and instructions regarding rituals.

Fire is an important element in Zoroastrian rituals. Zoroastrians are sometimes misunderstood as fire worshippers. Fire is used as representative of Ahura Mazda's light and wisdom. Zoroastrian temples are known as "Fire Temples" (*Agiary*).

Tower of Silence, Zoroastrian burial ground, Mazdanism, Yazd, Iran. Yazd is the cultural centre of Zoroastrianism.

The Parsee Diaspora

Due to Islamic persecution, some Persians left Iran in search of new places they could practise their religion freely. These groups have had to adapt or die out. Some migrated eastward in the ninth and tenth centuries AD and found themselves on the shores of Gujarat, India. The local king permitted them to stay, and this initial group formed the core of what has become known as the Parsee community of western India. This diaspora group is the main recognizable group that is in continuity with the original Zoroastrianism of Persia; the homelands succumbed to the pressures of Islam. Indeed they have become the group often first thought of when mentioning Zoroastrianism today. Parsee (Parsi) simply means "Persian".

THE MAGI

The Magi, or Wise Men, are perhaps the best-known Zoroastrians, because they are the ones who came to worship the infant Jesus, as recorded by Matthew in the Christian New Testament. These were probably learned priests, trained in the traditions of wisdom. The fifteenth-century mural below, from the Church of St Neophytos in Cyrpus, depicts the three kings following the star.

Religious Practices

Zoroastrianism is largely a religion without images, and is generally not very directive on its members. Zoroastrians do not have to worship in regulated ways. Prayer (invoking and celebrating Ahura Mazda) and ritual washing are practised: much of this is to do with purity and the desire to overcome evil. Ethics is foremost; followers strive to live a life of good words, good thoughts and good deeds.

One unique practice is the disposal of the dead. When a person dies, the body becomes ritually impure: death is the work of evil. Because the earth is pure, contaminating it with a rotting corpse or the ashes of a cremation would be sacrilege. Therefore corpses are laid out on specially built "Towers of Silence" (*dakhmas*) for vultures to devour. There is a special park in the city of Mumbai for this, but in other diaspora communities, Zoroastrians have adopted cremation.

THE TATA GROUP OF MUMBAI

In India, the Parsee community has done well for itself in business and in philanthropy. It is largely responsible for the very existence of Mumbai city, both historically and economically. This can be seen clearly in the Tata Group, which has been governed by at least five generations of the same Parsee family (Tata), and has grown to be one of the world's largest conglomerate companies, with interests in trucking, chemicals, retailing, energy, engineering, IT, hotels, steel, property, and services: it comprises 114 companies in 80 countries.

Sikhism

GURU NANAK, BELIEF, AND THE *GURUDWARA*

GURU NANAK

Sikhism is a relatively new religion. It was founded in the sixteenth century by Guru Nanak (1469–1539). "Sikh" means disciple, and "guru" means teacher. Guru Nanak drew on the main ideas of the day, bringing some synthesis to Islam and Hinduism, but in new and innovative ways. He expressed himself chiefly in poetry, which forms the basis of the Sikh scriptures.

THE SCRIPTURES

The Sikh scriptures are titled *Guru Granth Sahib*. Sikhism is based on the teachings of Guru Nanak (in the *Guru Granth Sahib*) and the nine Sikh gurus who followed him. The tenth guru – Guru Gobind Singh (1666–1708) – decreed that after his death, the spiritual guide of the Sikhs would be the book. No further gurus would come: the book itself should be considered as a living human guru.

The home of the Sikhs is the Punjab area of southern Asia. In 1947 Punjab was divided between the new states of Islamic Pakistan and secular India, and the Sikhs lost much of their homeland. In 1966, the Indian state of Punjab was divided again into three – Punjab, Haryana, and Himachal Pradesh – partly so that the Sikhs could be the majority in their own state, Punjab. There are between 20 and 27 million Sikhs worldwide, with between 60 and 80 per cent of these in India. Other significant populations exist elsewhere; for example, there are over 336,000 Sikhs living in the United Kingdom. In the United States, there are over half a million Sikhs.

Beliefs

Sikhism is monotheistic – there is only one God – and God should be kept in one's heart and mind at all times. One can recognize and experience God in the order of creation and in one's own heart and soul. Good actions rather than mere ritual are important: doing honest, hard work, treating everyone as equals, being generous, and serving others are the ways of a good life. *Karma* and reincarnation are still upheld, and the aim of Sikhism is to become one with God.

Guru Gobind Singh – Shaper of Today's Faith

The tenth guru, Gobind Singh, shaped the recognizable characteristics of today's Sikhism. In 1699 he founded the *Khalsa*, or the community. This is conceptualized as the community of "soldier saints". Gobind Singh founded the *Amrit* initiation, where initiates – both male and female – take new names and begin wearing the "five Ks".

THE "FIVE Ks" WORN BY INITIATED SIKHS

These five symbols have served to be strong elements of communal identification:

1. *Kesh*: uncut hair (Sikh men manage their long hair by wearing turbans)

2. *Kara*: a steel bracelet

3. *Kanga*: a wooden comb

4. *Kachh*: cotton underwear

5. *Kirpan*: a steel sword (used mainly for ceremonial purposes today)

A Sikh devotee tucks his *kirpan* into his turban during ritual bathing in holy waters in Amritsar, India.

Amritsar and the Golden Temple.

The *Gurudwara*

The sacred place for Sikhs is the *Gurudwara*. Literally, the *Gurudwara* is "the residence of the guru". Since the scriptures are considered to be a "living guru", the *Gurudwara* is simply a place where the guru lives: the only thing there is a copy of the scriptures. It is the presence of the *Guru Granth Sahib* that gives the building its religious status. Hence Sikhs go to the *Gurudwara* to learn spiritual wisdom by listening to the text being read or chanted. Surrounding buildings and rooms mean it is also a centre for festivals, weddings, and other community events. *Gurudwara* are now easily recognized in Western cities. In the United Kingdom, for example, there are over a hundred, and in California alone, more than twenty-five.

Daily *kirtan* or "worship" consists of readings from the scriptures (often singing, as the scriptures are mainly poetic), a sermon, prayers, and the communal eating of ceremonial food.

Amritsar and the Golden Temple

The city of Amritsar, and particularly the Golden Temple, has been the centre of Sikhism. This is where the scriptures are continuously chanted, and where pilgrims come to pay homage to the *Guru Granth Sahib* and to God. Due to the injustices done to the Sikhs over the years and the growing desire for a Sikh homeland, militants holed up in the temple in 1983. Indian Prime Minister Indira Gandhi ordered the storming of the temple, which consequently, due to Sikh rage, cost her her life at the hands of her own Sikh bodyguards in 1984.

Sikhs, Soldiers, and the Military

The Sikhs have been persecuted and variously shunted around their homelands over the years by Moghul rulers, Hindu kings, and then the British. The tenth Guru, Gobind Singh, made the militaristic notions of Sikhism more explicit: the Sikhs were to be "soldier saints"; they were to carry a *kirpan* (knife or sword), and their name after initiation was to be Singh ("lion"). After the injustices of British rule, and the Indian state's changing of national and state borders, the Sikhs ironically have found employment in both British and Indian armies. Much of this militarism is now ceremonial, and directed more to the conquering of the five inner vices of lust, covetousness, anger, pride, and attachment to the things of this world.

Japanese Religion and Shinto

OLD RELIGION IN A MODERN STATE

Like "Chinese religion", "Japanese religion" can be considered to be an umbrella category for the general religious ideas that are common in Japanese society. Buddhism (particularly Zen) and Confucianism are easily recognizable in Japan, but the distinctively Japanese religious tradition is Shinto. In a sense, "being Japanese" is informed by all three traditions.

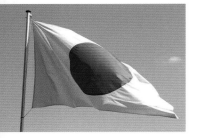

Shinto

Shinto has no founder and is not exclusive. It is a way of life: it is the cultural air that the Japanese breathe. Shinto does have explicit ethical principles by which a devotee is expected to live, but there is no list of commandments.

HOLY BOOKS OF JAPAN

The official holy books of Shinto are *Kojiki* or "Records of Ancient Matters" (AD 712) and *Nihon-gi* or the "Chronicles of Japan" (AD 720). The eighth-century date is significant as both Buddhism and Confucianism were well established in Japan by then. Hence these "holy books of Shinto" represent elements of all three traditions. In addition, they have a political role: the myths and stories therein endorse the ruling classes of Japan and promote Japan's supremacy over the peoples of neighbouring countries.

Kami

"Shinto" comes from the Chinese characters for *shen* ("divine being/deity") and *tao* ("way"); hence it means "way of the spirits". Invisible spirit beings and powers called *kami* are central in understanding Shinto. Shinto is ritualized devotion to *kami* and to *jinja* (shrines where *kami* live). *Kami* is not God, or gods: they are spiritually heightened human-like spirits associated with physical features of Japan. Hence Shinto is localized and can never be internationalized – it is anchored in the very physical landscape of Japan. *Kami* may be the spirit of a mountain, but it can also be the mountain itself. This localization means a multitude of local shrines, rather than a universally recognized or organized religion. Ritual at the shrines is more important than holding set beliefs.

The concept of *kami* is complex. Not all *kami* are good; some are evil. *Kami* means "that which is hidden", and therefore it can be regarded as the very essence of being of everything: it is the property of the sacred and mystical in anything – the spirit of that thing. *Kami* can also be anything experienced as strikingly impressive, or that has the quality of excellence about it, or that creates a sense of awe for someone. *Kami* is not God in the monotheistic sense, although the word has been used to translate the word "God" in the Japanese bible. This has caused some confusion for the Japanese, and misunderstanding for Westerners.

Some Shinto shrines and festivals have taken on a central role over the years. Festivals have the function of binding communities together. The spring cherry blossom festival – *sakura* – is popular today, and has ancient roots in predicting the harvest and announcing the rice planting season, by discovering the intentions of the *kami* of the cherry tree.

UNETHICAL BEHAVIOUR IN SHINTO

"Living according to the will of the *kami*" is perhaps the main ethical principle in Shinto; having a pure and sincere heart so that the *kami* are pleased is important. Bad living might include the following:

- upsetting *kami*;
- disturbing the ritual worship of *kami*;
- creating disharmony in the world;
- upsetting the natural world;
- disrupting the social order;
- bringing disharmony to the group of which one is a member.

LOYALTY

Shinto expects loyalty to community, and particularly to the group of which one is a member. This results in uniformity, and is partly responsible for a strong economic and industrial output.

Shinto and the Emperor

From about the sixth century AD it was widely accepted that the Japanese emperor was descended from the highest *kami*, the sun goddess Amaterasu, and that he was in contact with *kami*. This did not make the emperor divine per se (something often misunderstood in the West); rather, it meant that the emperor had an obligation to perform rituals to ensure the *kamis'* favour on Japan and ensure its prosperity. It was during the Meiji Restoration (1867–68) that the emperor took on divine aspects: before this, his status was ambiguous, with the country being run by *shogun* – feudal warlords. By the 1930s some were saying that the emperor was *akitsu mikami* – a "manifest god", and that Japan was a "divine country". Technically this meant that it was in the emperor that the qualities of *kami* were perfectly revealed, but no one was saying that the emperor was all-knowing or all-powerful. All sense of divinity – even if ambiguous – was suppressed after the Second World War. The nationalist and militaristic notions that emperor worship produced have been defanged: the emperor's role now is largely ceremonial.

LAND OF THE RISING SUN

Shinto scriptures are largely folk stories. They are heavy with political references: Japanese myths establish the powerful Yamamoto clan as descended from *kami* with authority to rule, and the rival Izumo clan as subordinate. Shinto myths largely agree that the Japanese are descended from the sun goddess Amaterasu: hence the symbol of the sun on the Japanese flag.

The iconic Mount Fuji (10,335 ft/3,800 m) is a *kami* in its own right, and the destination of thousands of Japanese pilgrims each year. The objective is to climb to the shrine on the summit: this entails an act of worship.

Bahai

UNITY OF ALL

The Bahai faith is a recent arrival on the world scene, founded in Persia (modern Iran) in 1863 by Bahá'u'lláh. In some ways it is an offshoot of Shi'a Islam, but it has gained worldwide presence, and members now number around 6 million.

Core Beliefs

The Bahai faith accepts all religions as true and valid. The core idea is that revelation is progressive: God has intervened throughout history at different times to reveal more of himself through his messengers. Thus Moses, Muhammad, and Jesus all reveal aspects of God. Therefore, even the Bahai faith is not the fullest and final: more is to come. All religions are of equal value, and unity is a key idea. Followers of Bahai believe that members of all religious traditions should work together for the common benefit of humanity.

PROGRESSIVE REVELATION

This sense of progressive revelation was heretical in the Islamic context of Bahai's founding: Islam claims that the Qur'an is the full and final revelation of God. Nevertheless, Bahai simply declare that their purpose is to know and love God. Prayer, fasting, and meditation are the means to this end. Their aim is to bring this simple message of unity to the world.

The Founding of Bahai: the Shi'a Context

Islamic scriptures speak of a "promised one", and in the eighteenth century a Shi'a Muslim, Shaykh Ahmad al Ahsai, founded a sect called the Shaykhi, instructing his followers to prepare for the "promised one". This was unorthodox, as it implies that the prophet Muhammad would have an imminent successor. Ultimately, one of these disciples, Mulla Husayn, a humble scholar, set out with his brother and nephew to look for the promised one in the city of Shiraz (southern Iran). Waiting outside the gates of Shiraz, he was approached by a stranger wearing a green turban, which indicated the stranger – Siyyid Ali Muhammad – was a descendant of Muhammad. He asked Mulla Husayn how he would recognize the promised one. Husayn's description fitted Ali Muhammad himself, and Husayn was persuaded he'd found the promised one. Ali Muhammad declared: "O thou who are the first to believe in Me! Verily, I say, I am the Báb, the Gate of God." This occurred on 22 May 1844, and Bahai believers celebrate this as the Declaration of the Báb: it is the beginning of a new era in human history. Ali Muhammad encouraged eighteen people to also declare their faith in him, the Báb. These believers were appointed as *Letters of the Living* and dispersed across Persia with the news that a new day of God had dawned. Persecution followed, and the Báb was executed in 1850.

Bahai house of worship, Wilmette, Illinois, USA.

The Visions of Bahá'u'lláh

After the Báb was executed, there was an attempt on the Shah of Persia's life, and a suspect, Bahá'u'lláh, a nobleman, was apprehended. In prison he had visions, which Bahai equate to the Holy Spirit coming on Jesus as a dove, or Muhammad's visitation by the angel Gabriel in the cave, or the enlightenment of Buddha. For Bahá'u'lláh it was the vision of a heavenly maiden promising a mission and help to unify all humankind. Hence the prison visions are central in Bahai: they are the manifestation of God. The actual assassin was apprehended, and Bahá'u'lláh was banished. This exile allowed a movement to grow by attracting disciples, but also because banishment spread this growing movement throughout the Ottoman empire – today's Iraq, Syria, Jordan, and Turkey. Bahá'u'lláh is God's messenger for this age. This was proclaimed at a garden in Baghdad, which has become known as the Garden of Ridvan (Paradise).

HOLY TEXTS

The writings of the Báb and Bahá'u'lláh are regarded as divine. However, because of the belief in progressive revelation, the teachings of previous manifestations of God (Buddha, Moses, Jesus, and Muhammad) are also regarded as divine revelations. Both the Qur'an and the Bible are considered to be authentic and authoritative texts. These are not seen to be in conflict, as it is understood that divine revelations are manifestations of laws and teachings appropriate for their own time. Because of the original Islamic context, Bahá'u'lláh refers to the Qur'an frequently. Nevertheless, on close reading, Bahá'u'lláh has been innovative with the text and original in many places.

Bahai Today

Bahai worship lacks ritual: there are no clergy and no sacraments. There are compulsory daily prayers, prayers at a funeral, and a simple marriage rite. Fasting is common: it represents the inner discipline of the soul so as to get closer to God. Simplicity and dignity are high values: Bahai are involved in a lot of social endeavours.

There is a celebration of community, with a strong emphasis on children. Children express the hopes of the unity of humankind. Festivals punctuate the year: Ridvan (21 April–2 May) is possibly the most important because it marks the declaration of Bahá'u'lláh as God's messenger in the Garden of Ridvan. One unique aspect of Bahai is that it allows local expressions, with little uniformity across the globe.

BAHAI TEMPLES

All Bahai temples have nine sides, representing completeness (the highest single digit number, in base ten). There are no images, statues, or pictures of deities in them, and no pulpits or altars. Reading and chanting of the world's religious scriptures is permitted, but no sermons are preached.

The Bahai Lotus Temple in New Delhi, India is the main temple for Asia. Its unique lotus flower shape has won architectural awards. It seats 2,500 and is open to people of all religions. It has proven to be a huge tourist attraction, competing in numbers of visitors with the Eiffel Tower and the Taj Mahal.

Mormonism

CHURCH OF JESUS CHRIST OF LATTER DAY SAINT

Members of the Church of Jesus Christ of Latter Day Saints (LDS) – or "Mormons" – consider theirs to be a restoration movement: God has restored the organization of the Christian church, along with its teachings and practices, after it was lost immediately after the time of Christ, due to humanity's disobedience. In essence, Mormonism claims to be the only true Christian church: true Christianity died with the last of the original disciples of Jesus, but has been restored through Joseph Smith's revelations in 1830, and the subsequent founding of the LDS.

Being a restoration movement Mormonism claims exclusive authority and priesthood to a new prophet (Joseph Smith) and his successors; it has "reopened the canon", that is, the authoritative core of writings, to be broader than the Bible; the Book of Mormon is the best-known new revelation.

Although American in culture and history, Mormonism has spread around the world and internationalized to a degree. It now claims 14 million members.

The Foundation of Mormonism

In western New York in 1823, Joseph Smith, Jr (1803–44) found Golden Plates allegedly outlining the history of peoples who migrated to North America from the Holy Land (modern Israel/Palestine) at the time of the Old Testament prophets. This was documented by Mormon, a prophet-warrior who was part of the Nephite people (Mormons believe the Nephites are one of the lost tribes of ancient Israel). Smith translated these and this became the Book of Mormon, published in 1830. Smith then founded a new church and people started to join. Much persecution ensued, however, and Smith was killed by a mob in 1844. He was succeeded by Brigham Young (1801–77). Although founded originally in New York, the Mormons moved west to Salt Lake City, Utah, by 1847. The shift west was due mainly to ongoing persecution.

AMERICANIZATION

Relatively isolated in Utah, the Mormons initiated several new things. Theocratic government (that is, direct rule by God) and new teachings emerged, some economic self-sufficiency was achieved, and new practices – such as the well-known "plural marriages" (polygamy) – began. Pressure from the state to conform to American institutions – both religious and civil – has meant that the LDS church has significantly revised or altogether abandoned some of these. In essence they have undergone a process of "Americanization".

Core Beliefs and Practices

While derived from Protestant Christianity, Mormons claim to be orthodox in belief and practice, yet are shunned by most Christian denominations because the Mormons do not hold to a Trinitarian belief in God. Three features dominate: male priesthood, the afterlife, and family. Priesthood is male, with several levels: "Elder" (often seen on lapel badges) is one of these. Salvation is open to everyone, but the level of heaven one can attain is determined by the quality and purity of life on earth. The priority of family demonstrates interdependency, and having numerous children shows the glory of God. Membership of the LDS is for people who accept the Book of Mormon as sacred, uphold moral lives, pay a tithe (10 per cent) to the church, and support the leadership: if these criteria are fulfilled, then attendance at the temple is permitted.

There is a strong millennial strand in LDS teaching: Jesus Christ's second coming will be in the United States, and the saints will then rule with him for a thousand years.

Left: Portrait of Joseph Smith, the founder of Mormonism.
Right: Manti Mormon Temple, site of the famous annual Mormon pageant, stands on a hill on the edge of Manti in Utah, USA. There are over 154 Mormon temples in the world. The temple is a location where various religious rituals are performed, particularly the endowment ceremony (ordination into service, with the empowering of spiritual gifting), marriages, and various rituals by proxy on behalf of the dead. The temple differs from the meeting house in which weekly worship services are held.

LDS SCRIPTURES

The LDS honours the following sacred texts:

- Old and New Testaments of the Bible

- Book of Mormon, subtitled *Another Testament of Jesus Christ*: the plates written by the hand of Mormon and translated by Joseph Smith

- *Doctrine and Covenants*: a special revelation that the prophet Joseph Smith received during a conference of elders at Hiram, Ohio, on 1 November 1831

- *Pearl of Great Price*: a selection of the writings of Joseph Smith, first compiled in 1851

Mormonism Today

LDS members are recognized by their public witnessing in pairs. Ordination of women was introduced in 1985, and both men and women must do two years' missionary service: this not only recruits new members but also "strengthens the testimony" of the truthfulness of the church and its prophetic origin. Additionally, most cities in the West have an LDS meeting house, which conforms to a similar architectural design world over.

Leadership has periodically been contested, with some splits occurring with offshoots that have very similar names to the original. Roughly half of the Mormons today are in America, and half in the rest of the world, with many in Spanish-speaking South America.

Mormons have gained some favour with governments, genetic researchers, and historians because they have built a large database of genealogies. This is due to the Mormon practice of praying for the dead, but it is a valuable global tool for assessing genetic traits and tracing family trees.

Brigham Young University in Utah is a centre of not only secular but also Mormon scholarship. Mitt Romney, governor of Massachusetts (2003–2007) and 2012 Republican Party candidate for the US presidency, is a Mormon.

Paganism

ANCIENT RELIGION IN A NEW AGE

The word "pagan" derives from the Latin *paganus*, meaning "village dweller", which in turn comes from the word *pagus*, meaning "rural". The term was originally used by the early Christians in the first century to signify "non-Christian", because Christianity, on the whole, was an urban movement around the Mediterranean. Regrettably, it then evolved into a negative term to mean "uncivilized" or even "Satanic".

Today, "pagan" is used to collect together a number of religious movements that honour nature. Adherents within these movements are comfortable with the title of "Pagan" and "Paganism". Paganism is increasingly regarded as an official religion, rather than a poorly defined adjective.

LUNAR AND SOLAR CYCLES

The lunar and solar cycles are significant: the solstice, equinox, new and full moons. Lunar cycles have been associated with fertility; hence there is a strong feminine motif throughout Paganism. Feminism and eco-feminism subvert a male-dominated world and the religions that claim only one God (who is usually male).

Core Beliefs

Paganism seeks to answer the following questions:

- How should we relate to the earth?
- How should we relate to other human beings?
- How should we relate to the divine?

These questions imply that humans' relationship with the earth, each other, and the divine is somehow out of alignment. In short, Pagans might answer these questions in this way:

1. We relate to the earth out of love of kinship with nature. We revere the life force and the ever-renewing cycles of death and rebirth in nature. We recognize that human life is intimately woven into the rhythms of nature.
2. We relate to other humans with a positive ethic. Each person is responsible for the discovery of their own true nature in harmony with others and the world. We need a tolerant, diverse, and humane society. Our motto is "Do what you will, as long as it harms none."
3. We recognize the divine, which is above and beyond gender. Deity has both male and female aspects. We therefore include goddesses and often feminize nature. We resist speculating about the nature of God.

Generally speaking, Pagans believe all of life is sacred. Similarly, they believe all of nature is sacred. Nevertheless, there are specific times and places that are significant to Pagans.

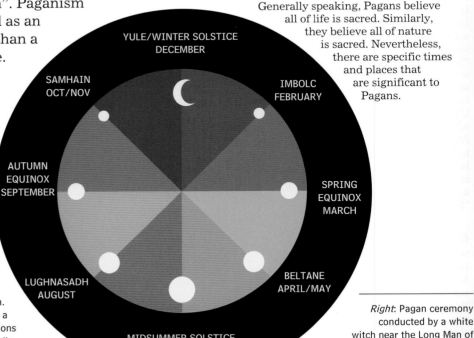

YULE/WINTER SOLSTICE
DECEMBER

SAMHAIN
OCT/NOV

IMBOLC
FEBRUARY

AUTUMN
EQUINOX
SEPTEMBER

SPRING
EQUINOX
MARCH

LUGHNASADH
AUGUST

BELTANE
APRIL/MAY

MIDSUMMER SOLSTICE
JUNE

Right: Pagan ceremony conducted by a white witch near the Long Man of Wilmington, Sussex, UK.

STONEHENGE

Stonehenge in Wiltshire, England, has had up to possibly eight developmental phases (depending on how the archaeologists interpret the evidence), but its current shape probably dates from around 3000 BC. Although the meaning of the site is contested, it is generally agreed that the stone circle served some purpose of astronomy/astrology, healing, ritual sacrifice, and burial. Various components of the Arthurian legends have been associated with the site. Although now tightly controlled due to the sheer volume of tourists, neo-Pagan seasonal (solstice, equinox) and druidic ceremonies are allowed at the site.

What Paganism is not

Paganism should not be confused with primal or indigenous religions. They do have some things in common, but generally, modern Paganism is a Western movement that draws on a number of different sources. In addition, Paganism is not Satanism. This idea is offensive to Pagans. Satan does not actually feature in Pagan worldview. Pagans will point out that it is Christians who have "Satan" in their worldview; real Satanists tend to manipulate Christian ideas. The association has been made historically due to linking the term *paganus* with "non-Christian", and things "non-Christian" were often deemed to be satanic during the Middle Ages; consequently, pagans were deemed to be devil worshippers. This confusion has been exploited in caricatures of witches and in various conspiracy theories, and the undisciplined use of the words "pagan" and "Satan".

GODS IN PAGANISM

While Paganism readily recognizes the deities (such as pixies, the Green Man, and faeries), they are not in cosmic struggle, nor is darkness and light contrasted, or good and evil. Nevertheless, balance, unity, and harmony are sought. Paganism is pantheistic (everything is divine) or panentheistic (the world is inside the divine, like a baby in the womb).

Who are the Pagans?

Paganism includes many solitary and private believers. Nevertheless, there is some order and structure. Three are noteworthy (and have many things in common), and a number of organized orders or societies exist.

■ Wicca: This is the "Old Religion", Witchcraft, or the Craft.

■ Druidry: This draws on the ancient traditions of England and Ireland, informed in part by the Celts. Druidry is officially recognized by the Charity Commission in the United Kingdom as a religion.

■ Heathenism. A modern expression of the Anglo-Saxon, Norse, and Germanic traditions in folklore.

Forms of worship and ritual vary enormously, but are usually associated with the seasons and with sacred spaces.

Postmodernity

CHALLENGE TO RELIGION

The world has experienced major shifts in key ideas during the twentieth century. One of the biggest shifts has been from modernity to postmodernity. This is not just a phenomenon of the West. With increasing globalization there is also increasing localization (or tribalism). These shifts affect us all.

Modernity v. Postmodernity

Modernity is a Western idea, and through colonialism, wars, and the media, it has come to influence much of the world. Social foundations used to be solid: today's realities and tomorrow's opportunities rested largely on reliable and agreed assumptions about God and science, and dependable state institutions and governments. However, from the mid-twentieth and into the early twenty-first century, this has eroded to an acceptance that there is not necessarily a "best" anything. We are now "post" – or after – modernity. These old, solid foundations of Western civilization are being re-examined, and in some cases challenged.

The "grand narratives" are the big stories and ideas that define a culture. Modernity was defined by a Judeo-Christian "grand narrative", and then overlaid with science. Reason was the defining way of knowing and learning. This is being broken down in postmodernity. Easy access to technology – the internet is an obvious example – means that a vast quantity of information is accessible to anyone. We are confronted with a huge array of consumer choices and religions: hence, religions of the world are now next door or at the click of a mouse. It follows then that the arts, politics, language – just about everything (including religion) – are accessible and can be challenged. Everyone's story is now equally valid and authoritative.

POSTMODERNISM'S KEY IDEAS

In *A Brief Guide to Beliefs* (2001), scholar Linda Edwards lists postmodernism's main ideas.

1. Objectivity and logic cannot be trusted. Truth is judged on how well something fits a context. Hence, religious texts can be challenged.

2. Specialist teachers should not be trusted. Authoritative religious teachers should be questioned – both those who speak and those who write.

3. There is no absolute Truth, only personal truths, all of which are relative to their context.

4. Tradition is no longer relevant because so much has been written excluding much human experience, particularly that of women and minorities. Events in history always occurred in a unique context.

5. The true meaning of words is now open for debate. Words are "heard" differently to what the author intended. Can the author actually intend any one particular meaning? Texts are in flux; meaning is determined by the reader, not the author.

6. The academic world is not the only place where new knowledge is birthed. Studying theology, for example, is seen as merely a way to create a privileged class of professionals to rule the church.

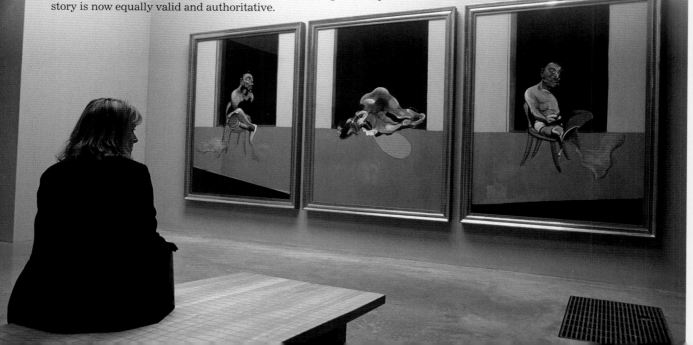

The *Matrix* trilogy explored postmodern
questions by drawing on themes from many
different religions, all in the context of a
sophisticated technology.

Religion in a Postmodern Age

● ●

While modernity and postmodernity may at first appearance seem to be
unique to the West, this shift also affects the whole globe. New spiritualities
are plundered from Eastern sources; a vast mixing of religions is now
possible.

1. In the postmodern age, Eastern
   religions are arriving in the West (for
   example Buddhism and new Asian
   religions), and Western Christianity
   has arrived in Asia and Africa; for
   example, Korean churches have
   adopted Western technologies, and
   prosperity theology (a contested
   Christian doctrine that material
   wealth is the will of God) has been
   beamed into Uganda from America.

2. The "Easternization" of religion
   is a feature of postmodernism.
   Christianity in the West is absorbing
   Eastern ideas; for example, this can
   be seen in the writings of Thomas
   Merton and Paul Tillich. Similarly,
   in Judaism this can be seen in
   the writings of Zalman Schecher-
   Shalomi.

3. Religions are becoming hybrids.
   There is much mixing going on
   both formally – as New Religious
   Movements – and informally, at an
   individual level. "Dual belonging" is
   now possible; for example, you can
   be a Jew and a Buddhist – a JuBu – at
   the same time.

4. Postmodern religion is characterized
   by a move away from official
   teachings. The Holocaust has caused
   a re-examination in Judaism as to the
   existence of God. The core teaching
   on suffering is being rethought in
   Buddhism. Miracles in Christianity
   are being challenged.

5. The rise of spirituality and the
   appreciation of life and nature
   as sacred are also features of
   postmodern religious thinking. Many
   people are happy to experiment in
   spirituality without committing to
   a religion. New personal identities
   can be built without having to be
   in a formal religion. There is a
   spiritualization of the environmental
   movement and feminism; Gaia is a
   female representation of the globe.

6. Religion is a commodity.
   Consumerism, the power of the
   media, and market ideology have
   reduced much in the world to mere
   products. Religion can be "shopped
   for": the rituals, the religious
   material, and the experiences of
   religion can be bought and sold.

Atheism, Secularism, and Unbelief

NO NEED FOR GOD

It may seem odd to include a section in a world religions book on atheism and various related views. However, these views often take the stance of "not-religious". In other words, they define themselves as against religion, giving tacit acknowledgment that religion is indeed the reference point.

Atheism

Atheism literally is *a-theism*, that is, "not-god". It is the absence of belief in any gods or spiritual beings. An atheist will not appeal to the will of God to explain the existence of the universe. Additionally, an atheist believes that a moral code for living can be devised without reference to a god or to holy scriptures. Census figures in Western countries demonstrate a lot of ambiguity about non-religious belief. In a sense, atheism has developed against Christianity. Atheism, then, is unbelief in the Christian God. Nevertheless, someone can be "religious" and atheistic at the same time. Buddhists are a good example. The Buddha himself was agnostic – ambivalent and uncommitted about the existence of an ultimate God. A Buddhist might argue that speculation about God is irrelevant.

Atheists argue that because everything in the universe can be explained in a satisfactory way through science and without using God as part of the explanation, then there is no point in saying that God exists.

Secularism

Many atheists are also secularists, and resist any special treatment given to religion. Secularists believe, for instance, that there should be no prayers in schools, and public funds should not support any one religion. Secularists note that a better future for humanity is in education and will oppose schools sponsored by religious groups. All people and all religions should be equal before the law.

While many secularists are atheists, some secularists are members of a religion. They don't think that belief per se is a reason for special treatment as, for example, political privilege. Secularism gained momentum in the nineteenth century as an explicit attack against the privileged position of the Church of England in the United Kingdom. Some secularists want religion to be a private matter for the home and think that the state should have no opinion or policy on it. They also seek to strip out aspects of culture derived from religion. Hence, popular Christian festivals such as Thanksgiving, Christmas, and Easter are becoming increasingly secularized, and it is common for those of all faiths, or no faith, to celebrate these holidays.

CHRISTMAS

The Christian festival of Christmas, which celebrates the birth of Jesus Christ, has become secular in many ways. Santa Claus, although originally associated with the Christian Saint Nicholas, is now an icon of the Coca Cola Company and has replaced Jesus Christ as the focal point of the holiday. The sharp division of church and state in the American constitution is another example of secularism: in state schools, prayers are not allowed to be said during school time. The teaching of the theory of evolution in Western education is sometimes offered as another example of secularism, especially if alternative possibilities of cosmic creation are excluded.

Two Important Questions

1. Why would people not believe in God, or be a member of a religion?

- They think there is not enough hard evidence to justify supporting any one religion.

- Religion makes no sense to them.

- They've been hurt by a religion.

- People sometimes simply accept the non-religious culture they live in.

- Religion doesn't interest them.

- They think they can live well enough without religion or God: religion isn't relevant.

- They hold that much harm in the world has been done in the name of religion.

- They believe that the world is a bad place, and therefore there can't be a God.

2. Do atheists and secularists think there is any good in religion?

- Many appreciate that religions have given beautiful art and music to the world.

- They acknowledge and appreciate some of the great religious narrative stories.

- They recognize that much charity work is done in the name of religion.

- They think that the scriptures of world religions are culturally very valuable, as moral teaching from any and all sources is good.

- They note that many "secular" proverbs have come from the religious teachings of the world.

- They acknowledge that religions value community and promote global harmony.

Religion as Psychology

Is religion a construct of our minds? Do we just need a really nice father figure in our lives to protect us from the scary world? Do we simply need someone to give us meaning and purpose? Maybe we have a psychological need to assure us that death is not the end, and hence our life here does actually have meaning? Because we are naturally fearful, do we need someone to look after us? Or is religion more than merely an outgrowth of human psychology?

VIEWS ON RELIGION

Karl Marx (1818–83), philosopher and political theorist, saw religion as a social tool used by capitalists to keep the working classes in order.

Sigmund Freud (1856–1939), famed psychotherapist, thought religion was like an infant depending on its parents for its needs. Ultimately religion was a delusion, but it did provide happiness and protection from suffering.

Ludwig Feuerbach (1804–72), a philosopher and anthropologist, said that belief in God fulfils certain societal functions. Humanity projected its own ideas about itself onto an imaginary supernatural being. God is a human invention.

Emile Durkheim (1858–1917), a sociologist, thought that religion is produced by human society, and has nothing supernatural about it. Religion promotes the bonds and relationships of society that give people meaning.

Friedrich Nietzsche (1844–1900), a philosopher, declared at the end of the nineteenth century that unbelief had killed off the Christian God. There was nothing left but despair.

Revivals and Renewal Movements

NEW RELIGIOUS MOVEMENTS

"New Religious Movements" (NRMs) is a term that originated in the latter years of the twentieth century as an alternative to "cult" or "sect". It describes a variety of new religious traditions deemed significant enough to be "movements".

Nevertheless, NRMs are rarely born out of nothing: some of the groups we have studied in this book could be said to be NRMs in so far as they sought to renew something that was perceived to have been lost in a mainstream religion. Examples include Bahai with Shi'a Islam, and Mormonism with Christianity. Even some of the older and now institutionalized religions, such as Christianity and Sikhism, could be understood to be "renewal" movements; for example, Christianity in Judaism, Sikhism in Hinduism, or even Buddhism in Brahmanism. This observation – that even renewal movements become institutionalized eventually – indicates that today's NRMs may end up being mainstream institutional religions tomorrow.

How Do We Categorize NRMs?

Terminology can be problematic in talking about NRMs. The word "cult" has connotations of "wrong" and "dangerous". "Sect" has been a less offensive word than "cult": it can equate to a new structural/institutional expression within a religion. Pentecostalism could have been considered a sect in its early days (from 1900s), but is now accepted as a denomination of Christianity. Soka Gakkai would be a sect of Buddhism in Japan, but could be regarded as a cult in Britain. The Jehovah's Witnesses might be regarded as a marginal Christian sect in the West, but as a cult in China. Some may call these "minority religions" or simply "heterodoxy", that is, beliefs outside the mainstream religion from which they were born.

Why Do NRMs Begin?

While the reasons for the birth of NRMs are complex, they could nevertheless be regarded as products of the tension between modernism and postmodernism. Secularism – keeping religion and the state separate – is one response to this tension, while the other is fundamentalism, a return to the perceived "fundamentals" of a religion in response to the overwhelming pressures and perceived threat brought by rapid global change. While some NRMs are fundamentalist movements, others are a response to the perceived dryness of secularism: there is a desire to make all of life sacred again. Some NRMs are birthed out of visions claimed by extraordinary people or their reinterpretation of holy texts.

SOME COMMONALITIES OF NRMs

1. An NRM is outside the mainstream in its beliefs, rituals, and community behaviours.

2. An NRM attracts converts from the indigenous culture – that is, the culture in which the NRM is founded. People join out of choice, not out of habit or culture. By the time the NRM enters its second generation, this dynamic changes, and children might be born into it.

3. An NRM often forms around a charismatic leader: this founder is usually leader for life, and then his or her legacy is passed on in some ritual lineage. The words and teachings of this charismatic founder become the core scriptures eventually, either claiming to be "new revelation" or gap fillers in existing religious literature.

4. An NRM is often apocalyptic. It usually sees itself as heralding a new age of human consciousness or history, either actually bringing it in, or predicting it imminently. In some sad cases, a whole movement has suicided when the hoped-for apocalypse failed. The People's Temple, with Jim Jones as its head, is a well-known example of this: in 1978, 919 people were found dead in Jonestown, Guyana, the victims of a mass suicide.

5. An NRM will offer a new way of salvation out of the perceived faults of this world. That new salvation is often related to the person or the teaching of the founder.

L: Jehovah's Witnesses at a mass baptism in the Atlas Arena in Lodz, Poland. *C*: A Jamaican Rastafarian. *R*: Hare Krishnas in Moscow.

How Should NRMs Be Classified?

NRMs could fall into one of three categories. In truth, any one NRM probably has characteristics of all three.

1. Those that embrace worldly things, and claim to make one a better citizen or better equipped to live well in this world. Examples include: Transcendental Meditation, Human Potential Movement, *est*, Silva Mind Control, and Scientology.

2. Those that reject or renounce the world. These groups tend to isolate themselves and have closed communities. Examples include: the Unification Church (the Moonies), ISKCON (the Hare Krishnas), Children of God (The Family), and The People's Temple.

3. Those groups that mainstream quickly and take on the characteristics of the dominant culture, such as Pentecostalism and the Charismatic Renewal Movements (both within Christianity).

Examples of NRMs and their Source Religions

With the name New Religions Movements, it may be wise to think of the unique "new-ness" of each religion, classifying it in relation to the source religion. In reality, most are a mixture, and some are informed by multiple sources (and could be "classified" by other categories)

NRMs informed by Christianity	NRMs informed by Hinduism	NRMs informed by Buddhism
■ Jehovah's Witnesses ■ Unification Church (the Moonies)	■ ISKCON (the Hare Krishnas) ■ Satya Sai Baba	■ Soka Gakkai (Japan, along with Humanism) ■ Falun Gong (China, along with Daoism) ■ Western Buddhist Order (Triratna)

SCIENTOLOGY

Scientology is a self-help quasi-religious movement founded in 1952 by L. Ron Hubbard (left). Using a system of belief and practice called Dianetics, Scientology is built on the belief that all people are immortal, and they have forgotten this, their true nature. Through a process of "auditing", people are rehabilitated from prior trauma in their lives to be freed into their true spiritual nature. Scientology has attracted a lot of attention due to its claims to be a science, its various questionable tax practices, and its affiliations with celebrities such as Tom Cruise.

New Age Movement and Esoterica

MAKING LIFE SACRED AGAIN

During the 1970s and 1980s, a number of esoteric movements found themselves grouped together in the Western media as the "New Age Movement". The word "esoteric" means "understood by a select few with specialist knowledge; private, secret and confidential; intended to be revealed to initiates only". It is perhaps a worldview rather than a formal religion.

These are not New Religious Movements (NRMs), but a collection of common impulses found in things as diverse as environmentalism, holistic medicine, feminism, self-help practices, magic, astral travel, astrology, tarot, crystals, channelling, and psychic healing. Western expressions are mixed in with Eastern elements, such as meditation, reincarnation, yoga, Zen, and *karma*. Some NRMs are categorized as "New Age" because of overlap in belief and ritual.

New Age adherents celebrate community using performing arts. Here people seek to explore a spiritual journey together outside the main constraints of institutionalized religion.

Is the New Age a Formal Religious Movement?

Actual conversion into one of the expressions of the New Age is not usually required, and hence it is difficult to count the number of devotees and adherents. Some expressions formalize themselves into organizations and institutions; others remain loose and fluid. Sometimes there are initiation rites, but often devotees are solitary, or only loosely connected. There is no core canon of scripture (although vast amounts of books are published), and there is no one founding member (although there are a number of gurus, psychics, and authors). It is diverse, relational, and networked, rather than organized and institutional. The New Age has a growing influence particularly in Western culture.

New Age Belief

The New Age sources itself from all of the religions: it mixes and matches, syncretizes, invents, and morphs into new ways. It represents a spiritual quest outside organized religion: spiritual wholeness is found by recognizing and harnessing the spiritual forces within oneself. It recognizes that the planet has reached a fresh stage of religious transformation: it is being transformed now, or is about to be. This transformation is related to humanity's divine potential to achieve wholeness, healing, and higher consciousness. The tools for this are taken from anywhere useful, such as ancient scriptures, experiences in nature, and the fellowship of likeminded people.

● SEE ALSO
SHAMANISM PP. 26–27
THE PEOPLES OF THE ANDES PP. 32–33
PAGANISM PP. 110–111
POSTMODERNITY PP. 112–113

Above: A New Age medicine wheel at sunrise with the Red Rock-Secret Mountain Wilderness, Arizona, USA, in the background. The medicine wheel has many symbols and can used as a tool for meditation.

A Visit to the Melbourne Mind, Body, Spirit Festival: The Author's Personal Testimony

I went to the Melbourne Mind Body Spirit Festival. The Exhibition Hall had 194 booths in it, and forty-nine psychics using tarot, crystal balls, and palm reading techniques to see into people's lives. I spent three days there, visiting as much as I could, and made these observations:

■ Monism – "all is one" – seems to be the prevailing ideology.

■ Cosmic energy pervades everything.

■ Personal empowerment can enter a person through the *chakras* – seven energy points along the line of symmetry in the body.

■ Meditation as a source of relaxation and re-centering is common.

■ There are a variety of spiritual masters. They are not as much divine as possessing extraordinary insight, wisdom, and energy.

■ Truth seemed irrelevant. People were more interested in finding significance for themselves, rather than asking "what is true?"

■ Spiritual experiences are important.

■ Ascension is expected: the ancient masters "ascended", and so can we.

■ The whole festival had a commercial feel to it. It was laid out like a supermarket. I was expected to pay for quite a few things: books, massage, healing sessions, teaching sessions.

James Redfield's Eleven Insights

Author James Redfield is representative of much New Age thinking and practice. His trilogy, *The Celestine Prophecy*, *The Tenth Insight*, and *The Secret of Shambhala* (Bantam, 1994–2000) were all bestsellers. The trilogy summarizes a common collection of "insights" that could be said to be shared among many adherents of the New Age.

1. A critical mass: A new enlightenment is upon humanity. This is based on a critical mass of people who have begun their spiritual journey.

2. The longer now: A more holistic and comprehensive worldview is replacing the older secular and technological ways of being of previous years. This new worldview is concerned with purpose, potential, and fundamental reality.

3. A matter of energy: The universe is not material; it is made of energy. Energy can be directed and projected so that there is an increasing flow of coincidences.

4. The struggle for power: Humans are marred by a desire to dominate; power usually hurts others.

5. The message of the mystics: Mystics and prophets of the past have taught us to connect with our divine energy within, so as not to be consumed by this hurtful power.

6. Clearing the past: As humans connect with this inner divine energy, there is greater awareness of having failed by taking energy from others.

7. Engaging the flow: A personal mission leads us to question, and this questioning leads us on a mystical path, informed by the wisdom of other humans.

8. The interpersonal ethic: When we help others, it increases the chances of synchronistic development in our own lives.

9. The emerging culture: If this all happens, then humanity will progress on its path of spirituality. We will be transformed and unite with eternity in a breaking of the cycle of life and death.

10. Holding the vision: Humans must therefore join together to uphold and maintain the spiritual vision. This vision has always been the unconscious quest of humanity.

11. Extending prayer fields: Humanity will join together in common spiritual vision when it depends more and more on prayer, positive thinking, and faith.

Fundamentalism

EXTREME RELIGION

Since the late twentieth century, there has been a significant rise in "religious fundamentalism". After the attacks of 9/11 (2001) on American targets, religious "fundamentalism" has often been portrayed in a negative light and is seen as one of the most threatening forces in the modern world. Many see "fundamentalists" as equating with Islamic "terrorists". But nothing could be further from the truth; fundamentalism in actual fact is a broad movement across many religions, and certainly not all Muslims are fundamentalists or terrorists by any means.

The Response to a Global Marketplace

The twenty-first-century world has become "smaller" than it once was; it is a vast global marketplace and melting pot of ideas and consumer items. As a result of colonial exploitation between the eighteenth and twentieth centuries, some have felt marginalized in their own religions and nations. Fundamentalism is partly a response to the threats of secularism and liberalism. Rather than opening up to new ideas, fundamentalism has constricted ideas into narrow frameworks. People have wanted to protect their beliefs and rituals in the face of perceived threats from the outside. Struggling and fraught adherents of a religion might come to feel powerless, and hence seek to preserve their distinctive identity. In addition, this is often a reaction to believers' experiences of prejudice and perceived persecution.

Protesters opposed to abortion demonstrate outside an abortion clinic in Belfast, Northern Ireland. Demonstrators like this are sometimes informed by "fundamentalist" interpretations of Christianity.

The Emergence of "Fundamentalism"

The term "fundamentalism" was first coined in California at the beginning of the twentieth century by Protestant Christian businessmen Milton and Lyman Stewart. These men were concerned with the emerging social and political liberalism they perceived in the society around them, and which, at that time, was prevalent within Christianity itself. They believed this thinking threatened both faith and morality. Their concern was to restate the central tenets – or the "fundamentals" – of the Christian faith, as they understood them. In particular, they upheld a belief in the literal interpretation of the Christian Bible.

As a result, they funded the publication of a number of small booklets for exactly that purpose. These booklets grew in number to a sizable collection of essays, which together were called *The Fundamentals* and which were published from 1910. However, the word "fundamentalism" has spread much more widely beyond this original context, taking on new meaning. It is often now used in connection with words such as extremism, militancy, tradition, conservatism, political/religious presumption, nationalism, secularization, right-wing politics, intolerance, and, as noted above, with terrorism.

Fundamentalism in the World's Religions

Today, in a broader sense, religious fundamentalism attempts to find the "essence" of a religion by appealing to its ancient sacred texts. The term is often applied to the "other" who is not understood, and whose lifestyle and politics are unacceptable to one's own interpretation of those texts. The label is used against those who wish to impose their views on others, and hence easily makes them feel inferior and dismisses them.

The carnage caused by the 9/11 attack on the World Trade Center in New York, USA.

"Fundamentalism" is a Trans-religious Term

Fundamentalism finds expressions in Islamic, Christian, Hindu, Buddhist, and Sikh thought – indeed in most religions, including New Religious Movements and even atheism. It can find expression in global arenas (such as the 9/11 attacks and in subsequent rhetoric and wars) or it can be regionalized (Palestine, Hindu political parties, and the Republican-Christian links in America, for example).

The "F" Word

- Fundamentalism is concerned with the scriptural roots of a religion, and also with religious authority. Fundamentalists often read religious texts literally, and may ignore the original context and intent of the scriptures. The interpreters of those religious texts (teachers, preachers, and writers) are invested with great authority. Fundamentalism seeks to claim the higher moral ground by attempting to return to the original and pure ideas of a religion.

- Fundamentalism can be understood as a reaction against modernism. Modernism has tended to disregard the sacred and the spiritual in society, and so fundamentalism is an attempt to reunite religion and society into a whole, and therefore to give people a sense of spiritual surety.

- Fundamentalism tends to define itself against the "other". If there were no enemy, then fundamentalism would cease to exist. The enemy can be conceived of as the radical questioning and the doubt of our age: fundamentalism claims that truth can be clear and known. It tends to see the world in black and white.

- The central beliefs of each fundamentalist religious movement are sourced from different religious texts and they seek different ends. Even within a certain fundamentalist movement of a religion, all adherents of that faith may not be in agreement as to motivation, ideology, and expected outcomes.

- Fundamentalist ideology is often millenarian; it believes that an ideal, or utopian, age is on the horizon, and needs to be ushered in by its true believers. This age is so imminent and the ideology so urgent that even violence is justified.

- Fundamentalist impulses exist in all religions. Additionally, secularism, the New Atheists, feminism, and other movements show signs of fundamentalism when they shut down dialogue and make exclusive claims to truth.

- Fundamentalism can be understood to be a worldview like any other: it seeks to tell a story that encompasses all truth and reality.

Bibliography

Ali, A. Y., *The Holy Qur'an: Translation and Commentary* (Birmingham: Islamic Propagation Centre International, 1946)

Arnold, E., *Bhagavadgita*, (Dover Publications, Inc., 1993)

Beaver, R. P., Bergman, J., Langley, M. S. et al. (eds), *A Lion Handbook: The World's Religions* (Tring, Herts, UK: Lion, 1982)

Bercholz, S. & Kohn, S. C. (eds), *Entering the Stream: An Introduction to the Buddha and his Teachings* (London: Rider, 1994)

Bosch, D. J., *Transforming Mission: Paradigm Shifts in Theology of Mission* (Vol. 16) (Maryknoll, NY: Orbis Books, 1991)

Chryssides, G. D., *Exploring New Religions* (London and New York: Continuum, 1999).

de Rachewiltz, I., *"The Secret History of the Mongols": A Mongolian Epic Chronicle of the Thirteenth Century* (Leiden: E. J. Brill, 2004)

Edwards, L., *A Brief Guide to Beliefs: Ideas, Theologies, Mysteries, and Movements* (Louisville: Westminster John Knox Press, 2001)

Flood, G., *An Introduction to Hinduism* (Cambridge: Cambridge University Press, 1996)

Green, J. B. & Baker, M. D., *Recovering the Scandal of the Cross: Atonement in New Testament and Contemporary Contexts* (Downer's Grove: InterVarsity Press, 2000)

Gyatso, T., *Freedom in Exile: The Autobiography of the Dalai Lama of Tibet* (London: Abacus Books, 1990)

Lewis, M. P. (ed.), *Ethnologue: Languages of the World* (16th edn) (Dallas: SIL International, 2000)

Lichtheim, M., *Ancient Egyptian Literature*, vol. 1 (London: University of California Press, 1975).

Mascaró, J., *The Upanishads* (Harmondsworth, England: Penguin, 1965)

Prothero, S., *God is Not One: The Eight Rival Religions that Run the World – and Why their Differences Matter* (New York: HarperCollins, 2010)

Redfield, J., *The Secret of Shambhala: In Search of the Eleventh Insight* (Sydney: Bantam, 2000)

Redfield, J., *The Celestine Prophecy: An Adventure* (Sydney: Bantam, 1994)

Redfield, J., *The Tenth Insight: Holding the Vision* (Sydney: Bantam, 1987)

Ruthven, M., *Fundamentalism: The Search for Meaning* (Oxford: Oxford University Press, 2005)

Sarangerel, *Riding Windhorses: A Journey into the Heart of Mongolian Shamanism* (Rochester, VT: Destiny Books, 2000)

Smart, N., *The Religious Experience of Mankind* (3rd edn ed.) (New York: Charles Scribner's Sons, 1984)

Smart, N., *The World's Religions* (Cambridge: Cambridge University Press, 1989)

Tweed, T., "Night-Stand Buddhists and Other Creatures: Sympathizers, Adherents, and the Study of Religion", in D. R. Williams & C. S. Queen (edn), *American Buddhism: Methods and Findings in Recent Scholarship* (Richmond, Surrey, UK: Curzon Press, 1999)

Tzu, L., *Tao Te Ching: The Book of Meaning and Life* (R. Wilhelm & H. G. Oswald, trans.) (London: Arkana/Penguin, 1985)

Index

A

Abraham 66–67, 69, 71, 74, 84, 88–89, 92–93
Aesir deities 21
Ahura Mazda 100–101
Al Aqsa mosque 67
Allah 41, 88, 90–93
Analects, the 61–63, 65
Ancestors, significance of 13, 24–25, 28–29, 31–32, 54, 59, 63, 96–97
Animism 12, 28, 87
Apus 32–33
Arhat 51
Ashrama-dharma 41
Atheism 114–115, 121
Atman 36, 38–39
Avatar 34–35, 37–38, 43
Axis mundi 27

B

Báb, the 106–107
Bahá'u'lláh 106–107
Bhagavad Gita 35–37
Bhakti-marga 35
Bible *see* Old and New Testaments
Bodhisattva 51
Book of Mormon 108–109
Books of Moses 67, 69–71 *see also* Old Testament
Brahma 22, 34
Brahman 36, 38–39, 43
Brahmin 23, 37–38, 40–41, 44
Buddhism, scriptures of 46, 48–49

C

Celtic gods 20–21
Chi 55, 58–59
Chuang-tzu, the 57–58
Confucian texts 55, 63 *see also* *Analects*
Confucius, exile of 60–61
Conservative Judaism 75
Constantine, conversion to Christianity 78

Council of Chalcedon 78–79
Covenant, God's 67–71, 80, 109
Cuzco 32

D

Dalai Lama 27, 44, 51
Dalit 38, 41, 85
Dao, the 56–58, 65
Dead Sea Scrolls 81
Dharma 23, 36–38, 40–41, 45, 47–50
Diwali 41
Dreamtime, the 29
Druidry 20, 111
Dukka 48
Durkheim, Emile 115

E

Egypt, gods of 17
Egypt, view of afterlife 16–17
Eightfold Path 45, 48
Enlightenment, the Buddha's 45
Enuma Elish 15
Epic of Gilgamesh 15

F

Feng shui 59
Feuerbach, Ludwig 115
Five Pillars of Islam 86, 92
Four Noble Truths 44, 48, 50
Freud, Sigmund 115
Fundamentalism, origin of 120

G

Geiger, Abraham 74
Gospels (texts) 76–78, 80, 93
Greco-Roman gods 18
Gurudwara, the 102–103
Guru Gobind Singh 102
Guru Nanak 102

H

Hadith 87, 90–91
Hajj 9, 88–89, 92
Harappan religion 22
Hare Krishnas 42, 117
Hasidism 75
Heathenism 111
Herzl, Theodor 74
Hijra 89, 92

I

Incan empire 32–33

J

Jainism, five vows of 99
Jainism, scriptures of 99
Jataka tales 48–49
Jati 40
Jen 63, 65
Jerusalem, significance of 71
Jesus, disciples of 77–78, 82–95, 108
Jesus, the messiah 76–77
Jihad 92, 95

K

Kaaba 88–89, 92
Kabbalah 75
Kama Sutra 42
Kami 104–105
Karma 23, 35–36, 38–39, 42–44, 53, 98–99, 102, 118
Khan, Genghis 27
Kosher 72
Kshatriya caste 37, 38, 40, 98

L

Lao-Tzu, founder of Daoism 56–57
Li 63
Luther, Martin 79, 84

M

Machu Picchu 33
Magi 101
Mahavira, leader of Jainism 98–99
Mahayana Buddhism 44, 49–51
Maimonides 70
Mana 13, 29
Marx, Karl 115
Mencius, disciple of Confucius 57, 61–62, 65
Mesopotamia, civilizations of 14
Mesopotamia, gods of 15
Modernity 41, 95, 112–113, 121
Moksha 36, 38, 41, 43, 99
Monism 35–36, 38, 52, 119
Mormon, the prophet-warrior 108
Mormonism, scriptures of 109
Moses 66–71, 74, 80, 93, 106–107
Muhammad, revelation of 86–94, 106–107

N

Native American rituals 26, 30–31
Nechung Oracle 27
New Age Movement 20, 33, 118
New Religious Movements (NRMs) 113, 116, 118, 121
New Testament, the 76–78, 80–82, 101, 109
Nietzsche, Friedrich 115
Nirvana 45, 48, 51
Norse gods *see* Aesir, Vanir deities
Numina 19

O

Old Testament 14, 68–69, 76–77, 80, 108
Olodumare 97
One Great Spirit 30–31
Orishas 97
Orthodox Church 79
Orthodox Judaism 75
Out-castes 38, 40, 85

P

Pachamama 32–33
Pagan, definition of 110–111
Parables, of Jesus 76
Parsee community 100–101
Passover 68, 73
Patriarchs 67–69, 77
Pentecostalism 84–85, 116–117
Postmodernity, key ideas of 112
Primal religion, characteristics of 13
Protestant Church 79, 85
Puja 35, 39, 98

Q

Qur'an 12, 86–94, 106–107

R

Rabbi Hirsch 75
Ramadan 92–93
Redfield, James 119, 123
Reform Judaism 74
Reformation, the 78–79, 84
Reincarnation 31, 35, 38–39, 42, 44, 51, 53, 96, 98, 102, 118
Religion, definition of 8–9
Resurrection, of Jesus 76–78, 80, 82–83
Roman Catholic Church 10, 79, 84, 96

S

Salafi 87, 95
Sangha 45–47, 49, 53
Schechter, Solomon 75
Secularism 9, 87, 95, 114–116, 120–21
Shabbat 70, 72, 74
Shaman 13, 26, 30, 32–33
Sharia 87, 95
Shia Islam 10, 94
Shinto, holy books 104
Shiva 22, 34–35, 42–43
Siddhartha Gautama (Buddha) 44–45, 48
Sin, introduction of 82
Smart, Ninian 13, 55, 123

Smriti texts 36
Spanish conquest, the 32
Sruti texts 36
Stonehenge 11
Pagans 110–111
Sturluson, Snorri 20
Sufism 94–95
Sunni Islam 10, 88, 91, 94–95
Sutras 48–49, 55, 99
Sweat Lodge, the 31
Synagogue 66–67, 69, 73, 75

T

Taboo 13, 29–30
Tai chi 58–59
Talmud 67, 70, 72
Tantra texts 37, 43, 51
Tao, the 55
Tao-te Ching 56–57
Tapas 99
Tapu 13, 29
Temple, destruction of 66–67
Ten Commandments, the 14, 68–70
Ten Plagues, the 68–69
Theravada Buddhism 49–51
Threefold confession (Buddhism) 47
Tibetan Buddhism 27, 49, 51
Torah 66–75, 93
Totemism 13, 29
Trimurti 22, 34

U

Upanishads, the 36

V

Vedas, the 23, 34, 36–38
Vanir deities 21
Vedism 23, 35
Vishnu 22, 34–35, 38, 41–42

W

Western (Wailing) Wall 66, 71
Wicca 43, 111
Wittgenstein, Ludwig 9
Wu-wei 58

Y

Yin and *yang* 55
Yoga 34, 42–43, 95, 118
Yoni-lingam 35, 43

Z

Zoroaster, prophet 100
Zoroastrianism, scriptures of 100

Picture Acknowledgments

Alamy: p. 15 Janzig/MiddleEast; p. 16 Ball Miwako; p. 19br Ilene MacDonald; p. 20 World History Archive; p. 21 The Art Archive; p. 25tr Robert Estall photo agency; pp. 28, 32 Deco; p. 30tl All Canada Photos; p. 31tr dynamitestockimages; p. 34 Art Directors & TRIP; p. 35t Morten Svenningsen; p. 35br Biju S.S.; p. 36 Travel Pictures; p. 37 Louise Batalla Duran; pp. 46–47 Phil Portus; p. 51 John Rodriguez; p. 53b Kelly Headrick; p. 55 BB Images; p. 64bl JTB Media Creation, Inc.; p. 75tl Eric Nathan; p. 76 UpperCut Images; p. 81 BibleLandPictures; p. 102tl Interfoto; p. 105 Adina Tovy; p. 114 Jeff Morgan 02; p. 117tm Michael Dwyer; p. 120 epa european pressphoto agency b.v.

Bridgeman: p. 45 Bonora; p. 82 Alinari

Corbis: p. 13 Paul C. Pet; p. 22 Paul Harris/JAI; p. 23tr Christophe Boisvieux; p. 23b Michael Freeman; p. 26 ILYA Naymushin/Reuters; p. 27 Alison Wright; p. 29tr Larry Williams; p. 30bl Ocean; pp. 31br, 84, 108 Bettmann; p. 40 epa; pp. 40–41 Frederic Soltan; p. 42 Pete Saloutos/Image Source; p. 43 Godong/Robert Harding World Imagery; p. 46 Zaheerudin/Webistan; p. 47 Kevin R. Morris; p. 48 Photosindia; p. 52 David Turnley; p. 59 Kevin Fleming; pp. 61, 64tr Imaginechina; p. 68 Roger Ressmeyer; p. 69 Mitsuhiko Imamori/Minden Pictures; p. 72 Evan Golub/Demotix; p. 73 Hanan Isachar; p. 74 Tom Hoenig/Westend61; p. 83 Oliver Weiken/epa; p. 85tm Jodi Cobb/National Geographic Society; pp. 88–89 ALAA Badarneh/epa; p. 92 George Steinmetz; p. 94 Bruno Ehrs; p. 99 Paul Panayiotou; p. 100 Raheb Homavandi/Reuters; p. 102br Bruno Morandi/Hemis; p. 104bl Jack Fields; p. 106 Lawrence Manning; p. 109 Nik Wheeler; p. 112 Sion Touhig; p. 117tl Grzegorz Michalowski/epa; p. 117tr Wolfgang Kaehler; p. 117bl Lebrecht Music & Arts; p. 119 George H. H. Huey

Getty: p. 49; p. 8l UIG; p. 19l Dorling Kindersley; p. 62 TAO Images Limited; p. 77 De Agostini

Glow Images: p. 12bl Werner Forman Archive/Tanzania National Museum, Dar es Salaam; p. 24 Werner Forman Archive/Private Collection; p. 33ml Therin-Weise/Arco Images; p. 53m Michel Setboun; p. 91 Werner Forman Archive/formerly Spink Collection

Lebrecht: p. 33tr De Agostini; p. 66 primaarchivo

Picture Desk: p. 8r Steve Raymer/NGS Image Collection/Art Archive; p. 18 Archaeological Museum Piraeus/Gianni Dagli Orti/Art Archive; pp. 25bl, 60 British Museum/Art Archive; p. 50 Stephanie Colasanti/Art Archive; p. 56 National Palace Museum Taiwan/Art Archive; p. 78m Cathedral of St Just Trieste/Collection Dagli Orti/Art Archive; p. 86 Manuel Cohen/Art Archive; p. 96tl United Artists/The Kobal Collection; p. 96br DANJAQ/EON/UA/The Kobal Collection; p. 113 Warner Bros/The Kobal Collection

Sonia Halliday: pp. 56–57, 70–71, 101bl

Superstock: p. 65 Eye Ubiquitous; p. 75tr Robert Harding Picture Library; p. 95 age footstock; p. 101t imagebroker.net

Topfoto: p. 33mr; pp. 9, 54, 90, 104tl ullsteinbild; p. 12tr Fortean; pp. 14, 17 World History Archive; p. 29bl Paul Ross; p. 31tl Topham Picturepoint; pp. 38–39 Dinodia; p. 58 Columbia Tristar; p. 67 Dan Porges; p. 78tr The Granger Collection; p. 81b Duby Tal/Albatross; pp. 85bl, 121 ImageWorks; p. 97 ImageWorks; p. 107 Hal Beral; p. 111 Kevin Carlyon/Fortean Picture

Maps and diagrams
Lion Hudson: pp. 40, 73, 80, 93, 110

Phoenix Mapping: pp. 14, 21, 28, 44, 60, 79, 88, 94, 97

Richard Watts: pp. 10–11

Lion Hudson
Commissioning editor: Ali Hull
Project editor: Miranda Lever
Proofreader: Elizabeth Hinks
Book designer: Jonathan Roberts
Picture researchers: Miranda Lever, Margaret Milton, Jonathan Roberts
Production manager: Kylie Ord

Other titles available in the **One-Stop Guides**:

The One-Stop Bible Guide
Mike Beaumont
ISBN 978 0 7459 5628 2

The One-Stop Guide to Christianity
David Winter
ISBN 978 0 7459 5323 6

The One-Stop Guide to Jesus
Mike Beaumont
ISBN 978 0 7459 5361 8

The One-Stop Bible Atlas
Nick Page
ISBN 978 0 7459 5352 6